COUNSE
AS A CHRISTIAN
CHALLENGE

ANDREW MONAGHAN

Gill and Macmillan

Published in Ireland by
Gill and Macmillan Ltd
Goldenbridge
Dublin 8
with associated companies in
Auckland, Delhi, Gaborone, Hamburg, Harare,
Hong Kong, Johannesburg, Kuala Lumpur, Lagos, London,
Manzini, Melbourne, Mexico City, Nairobi,
New York, Singapore, Tokyo
© Andrew Monaghan 1991
Print origination by
Seton Music Graphics Ltd, Bantry, Co. Cork
Printed by
Billing & Sons Ltd, Worcester

British Library Cataloguing in Publication Data
Monaghan, Andrew
Counselling as a christian challenge.
1. Christian church. Pastoral work. Counselling
I. Title
253.5
ISBN 0-7171-1831-2

The hard thing in life—which Christians believe can only be done with God's love—is to love one other human being with real unselfish love: the deep privilege, joy and challenge is to extend that love in ways both great and small to every human being we meet.

Contents

Acknowledgments

This book is dedicated to Gordon Joseph, Agnellus, Karl, Helen, Sheila, Claire, Anne and countless others who have mirrored in quite different ways, explicitly or implicitly, the sort of caring love that Christ came to make possible and that for me has a particularly precious incarnation in the counselling approach we are called to adopt to respond to one another's needs. Listening to one another—and listening to God in the process—allows us to grow together in love, no matter the misunderstandings or separations which make that journey difficult and indeed painful.

My thanks also to Michael Gill of Gill and Macmillan Ltd and to his painstaking copy editor, without whom this book would not have seen the light of day.

Introduction

IN HER powerful book on AIDS, Elisabeth Kübler-Ross makes plain her view that the ultimate betrayal for human society today would be failure to respond to the challenge of AIDS and care for the victims.[1] The purpose of this book is to suggest that for priests, ministers, religious and lay people, any failure to respond to the challenge presented by the dramatic growth of the counselling profession as the modern 'care-ers' would be the ultimate betrayal for Christianity today. A religion which Christ summed up as serving him in the hungry, the thirsty, the sick and the prisoners must, in my view, learn to serve people's needs with the skills elaborated in professional counselling. If it does not, it will not have listened to Christ's admonition that the children of the kingdom should learn from the children of the world.

The suggestion that 'life is our greatest teacher' and then that life should be the greatest teacher of the Church for its methods of communicating Christ's message would at one time have been regarded as heresy. This has changed, however, with modern biblical insights which start—as the pre-gospel preaching did—with Jesus as the real human being who himself learned from life, and then continue to see this process of human development of his understanding of himself and his message as the pattern which gives us real hope in our struggles to understand ourselves and what God wants from us. Christ's divinity, as ultimately witnessed by the New Testament, is the pledge that our journey is guaranteed by God's strength and guidance and not by our own.

The modern profession of counselling highlights the nature of this journey of self-understanding and development in ourselves and others. For those who believe that Christ and his Spirit are at the heart of life and human development in every human being, the listening and encouraging that are built into counselling are not just good human tactics for helping one another but a living out of the fundamental Christian message of being sensitive to God's presence in everyone. The question this book will raise is

1

whether twentieth-century life—with the Spirit and the risen Christ at the heart of that life—has been the Church's greatest teacher, or whether the Church has continued to live largely isolated and insulated from both the clamouring and whispering challenges of God's voice in the world and in people's personal lives.

A later chapter will reflect on the way Jesus related to people and yet another will survey the changes that counselling insights would bring even to the preaching work of the Church, but this opening section will examine the pastoral situations which highlight the very real dangers which emerge when good and well-meaning Christians try to care for others as Christ demands but ignore what are now well-accepted counselling principles. The dangers exist for Christian professionals such as priests, ministers, religious, elders and parish councillors; and they exist for the individual Christian trying to act in a fairly Christian way in the ups and downs of everyday life.

The fundamental argument of this book is that counselling should be the Christian response to cries for help in whatever form they emerge. This is quite different from but in our modern world a necessary preamble to the actual preaching of the Good News. Counselling is quite different—to go back to the early Church—from the kerygma itself, the first proclaiming of the Good News of the Resurrection, the gospel of hope for everyone, the announcing that death was no longer the final intractable barrier but rather the door to new life. It is quite different too from the Didache, the second oral stage in the spreading of the Christian message, the developed teaching that drew together the memories of the things Jesus said and did and began to elaborate them into persuasive presentations for different audiences.

We live in a culture that has been largely shaped by Christianity and in which the basic message of Christ is a given existential of our situation. It will never be fully understood, but it may well not be understood at all; and it may well have been rejected for a whole series of reasons which Christians can often sympathise with while still seeing them to be inadequate or plain wrong—but it is there. This fact alone changes the nature of what people look for when they look to priest, minister or caring Christian 'person in the pew'. They expect and indeed presume a witness to Christ's reality but because of past associations this comes across to them as a 'turn-off': one perhaps to be vaguely respected but one that at the same time often seems insultingly patronising. All that they are looking for in the first instance is a response to deep human needs which they themselves only partially glimpse. This was well summed up in a Feiffer cartoon where the long scrappy inquisitive one interrogated the old bearded searcher. 'What are you doing?' The old man replied 'I'm searching'. What for? An honest man? Money? Happiness? The list of negatives brought the exasperated question: 'Well, what are you looking for?' and the final sad reply: 'For someone to talk to'. The conviction which underpins this book is that people in our highly pressured and compartmentalised world are looking more and more for precisely that—someone to listen to them. Responding to that in Christian terms means something even more extraordinary: that is finding and listening to Christ in other people and doing it in the way which will most respect their woundedness and sensitivity.

Bishop Agnellus Andrew used to delight in using and expounding the saying: 'To speak is not the same as to be heard; to be heard is not the same as to be understood; to be understood is not the same thing as being accepted.' He would open it out into the distinction of proclamation, communication and persuasion in the Christian mission to the world. To this I would add the further guideline: 'To tell someone something is not as good as advising; to advise is not as good as counselling.' Both in terms of Christian caring and Christian communication, counselling would seem to be not only more appropriate but also more effective.

Precisely because counselling principles were ignored, one of the most damaging elements in my own training as a priest some thirty years ago was, I believe, the case studies into moral problems on which we thrived in what was then labelled the Moral Theology course. Human situations were outlined and we debated how general theological principles could be applied in those situations to provide neat solutions. I believe now that to come out of college expecting neat solutions to life's problems is a very real handicap, though in many ways, this was an invaluable teaching aid and one I am still grateful for.

In many modern study programmes the impression is given—rightly or wrongly—that the disciplined application of principles to human dilemmas has disappeared, and the disappearance

3

has engendered a bumbling and uninspiring vagueness in those entrusted with positions of moral leadership. It is sad to hear discussions about an issue such as euthanasia by people who have no idea of principles such as 'The end does not justify the means' (you can't take a life to alleviate distress); or the principle of double effect (you can relieve the distress even though the treatment also shortens life); or the principle of disproportionate means not being obligatory (you don't have to use extraordinary means to preserve life where all reasonable quality of life is irretrievably at an end). It's hard enough to get agreement even with such clear starting points but is almost impossible without!

The danger, however, in the old training such as I experienced was that leaders emerged who were eager to communicate 'moral solutions' and saw this as the specifically priestly or religious service they could offer to a people searching for definite moral guidance, for answers to the major human dilemmas of life. Modern study into the psychology of human relationships has combined with the new theology of Christ's incarnation to emphasise that people are damaged by the immediate presentation of even the right solution. It contradicts the nature of true human communication, it violates the respect Christ inculcated for the mystery of God in every human being—and it stultifies that learning process in the care-ers which alone can equip them to serve human needs.

Many would argue that 'life is our greatest teacher' in the sense that learning from experience counter-balances any theoretical problem in pastoral approach. It is of course true that life is our greatest teacher but this is very far from solving all the problems. Some understand the dictum as demanding an attack on all intellectual activity, theology and principles: this is the foundation for the all too common caricature or self-projection of the priest or minister as anti-intellectual. How many have we met who are almost ashamed to have been caught reading a serious book of theology? Or how many are never likely to be caught in such a crime? And yet these are the ones entrusted with preaching the Word of God in season and out of the season and with being opinion leaders in the sense expounded by Pope Pius XII. Their excuse that life has taught them all they need to know is a hollow self-deception and an insult to God's choice of them to communicate the Word of God.

4

Others would argue very profoundly that life as our greatest teacher is the logical conclusion from belief in God's presence in ourselves. If God's Spirit is working with our spirit, then listening to that Spirit, listening to God is seen as one of the main purposes of prayer and the spiritual life. As such, it is seen as eliminating human techniques both for communication from within to the outside world, and for receiving. Here, however, the old adage comes into play: 'We must work as if it all depends on us and pray in the knowledge that it all depends on God.'

Lastly, as already indicated, the belief that 'life is our greatest teacher' draws significance from the words of Jesus that 'in so far as you did this to one of the least of these brothers of mine, you did it to me' (Mt. 25:40). The belief that we find and serve God in the needy is the ultimate challenge of the Christian faith and the ultimate meaning of the Incarnation and Resurrection. As Karl Rahner put it: 'This is the ultimate truth because God himself has become our neighbour and so in every neighbour it is always he, the one who is always nearest and most distant, who is accepted and loved.'[2] Thus St Augustine can say 'If you love the members of Jesus Christ, then you love Jesus Christ; in loving Jesus Christ you are loving the Son of God and in loving the Son of God you are by that fact loving the Father. This love can admit no division.' St John Chrysostom says to divide the two is like trying to divide soul and body in man. Von Balthasar says 'Christ and the Church are one flesh, they must never be separated.'[3] Louis Evely points out the Nestorianism of those who exclude Christ from the world: 'They put him in heaven and burn incense to him and get him out of the way, then the commandment of love of neighbour is only a mere test of love, an opportunity of merit.'[4] You might feel he is exaggerating the picture but I'm sure many of us will recognise the sort of spirituality which misses the real point, namely that we must instead serve Christ in that neighbour and love him.

Fortunately, modern spiritual books are full of this approach. Eamonn Bredin sets the scene in a very moving passage in *Disturbing the Peace*:

> Jesus breaks open systems that exclude and declares that disciples are to take the initiative and make themselves neighbour, sister, brother to those who are excluded or marginalized.

People can be truly free only if they are together in a new way, serving the needs of the other. This is what he enfleshes in his own scandalous solidarity with outcasts and sinners. Thus he becomes the living parable of the kingdom of God.[5]

The popular spirituality of Michel Quoist in *Prayers of Life*, *The Christian Response* and *Meet Christ and Live* expounds that parable and so also does the more recent book of his radio and television scripts. For him the other is 'our daily bread, our Eucharist. He lives in the same house with us, works in the same office, rides the same bus, sits beside us at the pictures. The other's name— Jesus Christ.'[6] Christopher William Jones in *Listen Pilgrim* is another outstanding example of this approach:

This is the other part of being a Christian: to accept people as they are, for what they are, the bad and the good, to accept them immediately, no matter what you learn about them later; to bear their burdens if they are heavy or if they are light, to walk the way of the cross with each Christ we meet.'[7]

Lastly Louis Evely:

'What the Incarnation above all reveals is that we are so poor that the whole of God's love within us is not too much to help us begin to love husband and wife, children, work, friends as they need. One must be God to give us a sufficient motive for loving him, to give us a reason proportionate to the immense sacrifices and terrible disappointments such a love involves. The only way to love man is to believe God is man.[8]

All three aspects of 'life as our greatest teacher' have been significant for me in my years as a priest, a teacher and a somewhat amateur radio counsellor. I suggest they may well help us explore the reasons why counselling should be the characteristic of Christian care-ers.

When it comes to questions of defining what counselling is, I am reluctant to engage in definitions—since others have done this better that I ever could—but I use it in its normal modern sense of that approach to people coming with problems which seeks to listen rather than give instant advice or solutions, and which is non-judgemental (and in this sense non-directive), rather than either handing out to people assessments of their inner worth or even defining that person's inner status or failings in neat little labels to ourselves. Counselling rather than pontifical advising is an attitude first and foremost, and from that attitude stem the practical techniques which are being expounded more and more by others far more competent than myself. I hope my own attitudes will emerge from the book, but perhaps at this stage I could mention three works I believe are outstandingly useful.

The first is the broadly based *On Becoming a Counsellor* by Professor Eugene Kennedy of Loyola University, Chicago.[9] It is intended for 'those who, without extensive psychological training, must deal with troubled individuals'. He outlines well that counselling means entering into a relationship, a relationship which demands awareness of the thoughts and feelings in both counsellor and counselled which will affect and form the interaction. Counsellors will need support themselves if they are to be constructive and not damaging supports for others. They will have to recognise the limitations of their counselling and work easily and willingly with other health-care professionals but, within those parameters, will be able to develop from a basis of common sense, sensitivity and respect very real skills in making this listening active and constructive.

It is at this point that I find Ronald B. Adler and Neil Towne's book *Looking Out, Looking In* particularly valuable: Chapter 6, 'Listening versus Hearing' is for me the core of the book.[10] They speak of pseudo-listening, stage hogging, selective listening, insulated listening, defensive listening, listening in preparation to ambush the unwary confidante (perhaps the principal clerical fault!) and insensitive listening; but then move to outline the distinction between passive listening and the active listening which turns our listening into counselling when we either simply reflect back to people in a warm way our acceptance of what they are saying or—when the time is right—help them to interpret what they are saying by summarising what they've said or even paraphrasing the unstated feelings which lie beneath what has been said.

For Christian care-ers, Howard J. Clinebell's book *Basic Types of Pastoral Counselling* has become an important textbook.[11] He gives in useful diagrammatic form a model which at the very least could serve as a starting point for constructing our own personal vision of how counselling is a Christian challenge for all of us today:

Pastoral Care Function	Historical Expressions	Contemporary Counselling Expression
Healing	Anointing, exorcism, saints and relics, charismatic healers	Depth counseling (pastoral psychotherapy); spiritual healing
Sustaining	Preserving, consoling, consolidating	Supportive counseling; crisis counseling
Guiding	Advice-giving, devil-craft, listening	Educative counseling short-term decision making; marriage counseling
Reconciling	Confession, forgiveness, disciplining	Confrontational counseling; superego counseling; marriage counseling; Existential counseling (reconciliation with God)

1

Life Situations Challenging the Christian Care-er

IN SOME WAYS, every human situation is so much a mixture of many issues that labelling or categorising problems is dangerous. It militates too against Christ's care for the individual ('every hair on your head has been counted'). Yet common characteristics do mark some major areas of our journey through life and this chapter will look at a number of the main ones. Having said that, however, the Christian priest, minister, religious or concerned lay man or woman will have to be continually sensitive to the fact that any one person in a given situation will also be affected in that situation by everything else in life up to that point!

Bereavement

At first sight, this would seem to be the area of pastoral need which is most open to the proclamation of the heart of the Christian message: that death leads to new life. Here we have a dramatic paradox. On the one hand, it can be argued that Christianity has lost its bite precisely because it has failed to proclaim the hope that rests in a future life. On the other hand, its too glib proclamation of a future life—to comfort the bereaved—has often provoked deep resentment. Marxists inspire immense commitment and dedication (witness the financial and time sacrifices made by members of Marxist political cells) in many people who believe that they will never share in the fairer future they are giving their lives to build. Yet it is their vision of the evolving future and the satisfaction of playing a positive part in constructing that future which gives them the strength and energy to go on. The Christian Churches have often been less effective in conveying their vision of the 'already' of what Christ has achieved in giving us new life and the 'not yet' both in this world and the next which we are given the opportunity to help build. They have failed to communicate that the heaven preached is not a matter of sitting in a white nightshirt on a cloud plonking a guitar for all eternity but rather of what St Augustine described as 'enjoying others in God'. This insight is immediately understandable to the bereaved and can be an immense strength. In consequence, the Christian faced with someone broken by the loss of a loved one almost instinctively longs to speak of 'a new closeness to our loved ones who have died' or to say that 'God wanted our loved one to be happy with him'. These, however, may not be the things we should first say and the saying of them can often have the opposite effect from the comfort and reassurance intended.

This is true even in the light of the new insights from modern theology which have removed some of the worst obstacles. No longer need we wheel out the discredited theory of Limbo to explain the apparent contradiction between God's wish 'to save all' and the apparent universalism of 'Unless a man is born again of water and the Holy Spirit, he cannot have eternal life.' The mother grieving a child who died before Baptism only wants to know whether she can think of her baby in heaven or not and whether she will see the child again or not.

Ladislaus Boros' theory of death as final decision is far from certain and far from solving either the grieving mother's problems or those of theology. Nonetheless, it leaves the mystery where it should be—with God and his universal love. Seeing death as final decision does make a more immediately direct and helpful first insight to share with the bereaved mother or with anyone mourning a loved one. To quote him directly: 'Death gives man the opportunity of posing his first completely personal act: death is, therefore, by reason of its very being, the moment above all others for the awakening of consciousness, for freedom, for the encounter with God, for the final decision about his eternal destiny.' Boros is useful too for his neat turn-around of the last page of André Malraux' Man's Estate. This was intended as an expression of the futility of life, but Boros uses it to set the scene for the Christian teaching that death and all involved in it in fact gives meaning to the whole of life. Listen to Malraux about the old couple sitting on either side of the fire: 'You know what they say "It takes nine months to create a man, and only a single day to destroy him." We both of us have known the truth of this as well as anyone could ever know it. . . . It does not take nine months to make a man. It takes fifty years, fifty years of sacrifice, of determination, of so many things! And when that man has been achieved, when there is no childishness left in him, nor any adolescence, when he is truly, utterly, a man—the only thing he is good for is to die.' Despair then or the richest hope![1]

Any bitterness involved stems from man's universal experience of losing what is most rich in life: 'What is painful in death is that in its dark inflexible shadows and vagueness, it seems to deprive us of the very richness of our human personalities which through life we have felt maturing to a consciousness of immortality.'[2] As St Paul emphasised, death remains the last of the enemies of mankind that Christ triumphs over (See 1 Cor. 15: 16). Death needs courage, for as Barnabas Ahern puts it: 'Death involves a process of being unclothed, of having the securities of life as man knows it ripped away. Death, even at best, still looms as an exile from all that is familiar.'[3] Now the point is that death even for the devout Christian who is bereaved is just as traumatic because it is just as much a barrier, just as much a ripping away as death is for the one dying. The sad thing is that Christians often feel guilty because they cannot feel good about the death of their loved ones; and because they feel guilty, they can be badly hurt.

In the Roman Catholic Church, the suggestion after the Second Vatican Council is that the funeral service should be a celebration of the resurrection Christ makes possible. This is of course the all-important truth which must be embodied in a funeral service, but the way we do it will determine whether real hope is communicated or whether all hope is destroyed because there is no prior acknowledgement of the bereavement, the ripping away, the separation, and the last enemy of mankind that has still to be overcome by living through our share in the sufferings of Christ. The number of those damaged by a cheerful cleric 'celebrating' their loved one's departure to another life is much greater than those damaged by an inadequate liturgy which failed to point properly to the Resurrection as it should.

All the modern studies of bereavement have emphasised the reasons for what most sensitive priests learn very quickly in terms of sensitivity by living through bereavement with their parishioners. The only exceptions seem to be the enthusiasts at either end of the emotional spectrum of modern spirituality: those who rely too heavily on creating a religious experience of joy and those who are too visionary to include any mere human emotion. There are differing analyses among the experts but all agree that bereavement is a process, with stages that have to be worked through. Colin Murray Parkes is fairly typical in suggesting that there are four phases in the process of grief: numbness, pining, depression and recovery; and the powerful emotions experienced during the journey towards recovery can include a sense of stigma, anger even at the loved one for dying, guilt for feeling that way and deprivation in the sense of missing all the practical things that the person who died represented. Each and every one of those emotional reactions must be given due respect and place. Each and every phase represents an emotional block which must be listened to, acknowledged and reverenced in turn before the communication of the message of Christian hope is shared.

The numbness at the beginning is a mixture of panic and an inability to feel anything. People can even feel guilty about that. This is followed by the pain of pining for the loved one, a true physical pain that leads to a lack of acceptance of the fact of death, or a desperate search for the loved one and for the redefinition of the person's whole identity which has been destroyed by the bereavement.

Depression—the next stage—is now well accepted as a very real disabling phase of life that can be described as a temporary or very much long term illness. There are two forms, the endogenous, which links in with hereditary and early development factors, and the reactive which is triggered off by a life crisis such as bereavement (or a series of such crises). Both separate the victim from hearing and responding to the outstretched love of those around who care (including the caring Church) and prevent the energy which would allow the victim to do the practical things which allow life to continue.

Lastly, there is the painful road to recovering coping mechanisms, a road which has to be carved out of the thickets represented by the stigma felt in such experiences as being a widow or widower in a society centred on couples, or merely from being sad in a western world in which mourning is treated as though it were a weakness; and by the insecurity which arises from being deprived of all the practical supports that once were provided by the loved one (he always saw to the bills, she always did the cooking etc).[4] Our relationship with the Christ who has gone before us and walks now with us will help at each of these stages but should not be allowed to eliminate them. If they are eliminated, if emotionally based religious experience enables us to jump some of the stages to what seems to be the last stage of acceptance, then those missed-out stages of anger, 'if only' and depression will recur later on—perhaps in disguised forms—and cause greater havoc still.

When it comes to the anger and guilt on the way towards the recovery stage of mourning, the Christian response can be particularly unhelpful. Preaching tends to say that anger is wrong, that anger against God is evil and that anger should be avoided at all costs. Counselling respects the mystery of the human being coping with grief and is supremely conscious that anger as a reactive emotional state has to be distinguished from emotions deliberately left to run riot, no matter who they hurt, or even directed maliciously with the precise purpose of hurting others. Such is sin, the other is a healing response to pain. Here those psalms which allow us to express an irrational anger against God provide an important vehicle of healing prayer. Guilt emerges either from feelings of 'If only I had said' . . . 'if only I had been'—or from the feeling that we should have died rather than the person who in fact died. Here again, any attempt to apply Christian forgiveness to that guilt serves only to reinforce what is false guilt, a set of feelings which have to be talked through and thus dissipated by being seen in context instead of assuming undue significance by being trapped inside one's own thoughts.

Depression

'You must give yourself a good shake' is often paralleled by statements such as those which suggest that depression is a result of a lack of faith or trust. It is to be hoped that Christians have moved away from thinking that to appear fed up is a contradiction of Christian joy, a sure sign that we have neglected our prayer life or have been abandoned by God. Nevertheless, depression is often so isolating and so inward that it can be increased by a priest or minister who feels threatened if there is no response

13

from the person they are trying to help. Both end up feeling a bit of a failure, one because of the lack of response and one because of the conscious failure to provide the response which would make caring Christians feel they had achieved something.

The working distinction has been made between endogenous and reactive depression. Some would argue that all depression results from traumatic events rather than heredity. In some ways this is irrelevant because there will always be associated events which can be opened up and help the healing process. Clearly it is not for the care-er to decide the medical diagnosis as to whether there is the illness of depression or whether the person is fed-up or anxious or worn out or burned out or self-obsessed. Again too it is for the doctor to decide on the wide range of anti-depressant drugs or ECT treatment in severe situations: I am presuming that there will be a referral to medical help—in addition to or along-side the counselling—whenever the person's normal coping mechanisms are not functioning i.e. when they cannot continue their ordinary routine. Not everyone agrees that there is a clear distinction between endogenous and reactive depression, but this does not change the general agreement that it is important to look at the elements where it is clear that we're reacting to recent traumatic events, and at the areas where we are affected by all the undervaluing of ourselves by ourselves and by others which has taken place over the years. Many feel that there is a chemical imbalance at the root of at least some forms of depres-sion; others feel that there is always a chemical element as yet unidentified. Again too, it is clear that there is a range of illness covered by the term depression. At one end is what Dr Jack Dominian of the Central Middlesex Hospital describes as a nor-mal necessary experience, 'a kind of human radar which scans the reality of life and gives our appropriate response'.[5] At the other extreme, there is psychotic depression which is a very definite collapse of all ability to cope and often results in bizarre and alarming loss of contact with reality and even the small practicalities of life.

What for me makes the problem worse is the confusion between what spiritual writers call the 'dark night of the soul'—a spiritual condition or trial from God depending on your reli-gious attitude—and the illness. Both St Theresa of Avila and St John of the Cross would arguably now be described as suffering from depression. St Ignatius undoubtedly so. So also Martin Luther and John Calvin. Many of the world's geniuses suffered similarly. Isaac Newton, Beethoven, Darwin, Van Gogh, Tolstoy, Churchill and Lincoln. J.B. Phillips was so unable to shake off depression that he had to resign his first living and go into hiding, where he corresponded with other depressives such as Leslie Weatherhead who had two hundred hours of analysis and took a drug before preaching on a Sunday. The hymn-writer William Cowper tried to kill himself several times. C.H. Spurgeon preached his best sermons in the depths of depression. The list makes one wonder whether this is the reason there are so many dreary sermons! More seriously, the frequency of depression in religious people gives substance to the belief in some psychiatrists that religion's emphasis on self-examination and awareness of guilt can encourage the factors which lead to depression and make it take root.

All this leads me to believe that the Christian outreach to the depressed must be extremely cautious and careful. When some-one is suffering from loss of appetite or weight gain, has sleep difficulties, is constantly fatigued and agitated or easily irritated, has clearly slowed up in doing even ordinary things, has difficulty concentrating, feels guilty and experiences haunting death wishes or actual thoughts of suicide, that person would seem to be de-pressed. Yet all these characteristics are often identified by reli-gious people as sinfulness or sloth! They must be encouraged to stop thinking of spiritual weakness and pointed to acceptance of illness as the reason for the malaise. In *Listening to Others*, Joyce Hugget speaks of how her doctor prescribed anti-depressants:

> Anti-depressants! I dared not admit to anyone that I had a bottle by my bedside. I felt so guilty. And a complete failure— as a clergy wife, a mother and a Christian. And I felt angry with myself for being feeble enough to be incapable of coping. Now whether anti-depressants are necessary is a medical deci-sion (as also ECT for a quicker answer in severe cases) which should be made in consultation with the patient, but the Christian response for me must be a clear teaching that depression when diagnosed medically is an illness and that ill-ness is a random occurrence in the human condition that is not 'willed on us by God', that is in no sense a 'punishment for sin or failure to be what we should be'.[6]

Christian faith believes that Christ can heal but the choice of who is healed is not dependent on our deserving or not deserving healing. Any suggestion that if we do this and don't do that God will intervene into the laws of nature to heal us is extremely dangerous because it leads to the opposite conviction that if we're not healed, then we've sinned or worse, are 'possessed by the devil'.

Much good has been done recently in a negative way by Evelyn Waugh and more positively by brilliant broadcasters such as Rabbi Lionel Blue and Gerald Priestland who have spoken so movingly of their illness of depression. Their ability to speak effectively of religious conviction co-existing side by side with depression must have encouraged many in their quite different ways. They witness clearly, however, that the clumsy 'religious encourager' gives them very great pain indeed when they don't first listen before speaking. It's only too easy with those who are depressed to forget the anger which may be disguised by their calm. It's very difficult at times for the person wishing to help to avoid the pressure to give those who are depressed a good shake, and it's immensely irritating to have to cope with what is often a desperate desire for affection pulsing away under a severe outward inability to accept affection. Those who suffer from depression are challenges to Christian patience rather than Christian enthusiasm if their very personal qualities and sensitivity are to be set free. The cheery preacher of God's joy inflicts immense pain!

Guilt

This section will be a little more detailed since problems of false guilt often make healing from depression and bereavement more difficult for religious people. The Christian care-er will need to develop sensitivity to the existence of false guilt in those needing help, and will need to work hard to avoid reinforcing false guilt by using the language of the real guilt which Christianity tries to counter.

A) 'False' and 'True' Guilt

'A feeling of guilt follows every person like his shadow, whether or not he knows it.' Thus Edmund Bergler, a psychiatrist. The problem for the Christian response is that guilt can either be

16

appropriate, when a person is aware or becomes aware of doing wrong; or it can be false guilt, arising from conditioning or from neurotic weakness of one kind or another. Many books have been written on the subject of false guilt, the human reaction to situations of pain which leaves us feeling dirty, convinced we're failures, feeling ourselves convicted of being as bad as we always knew we were or as we've always been labelled, and so on. The classic sort of example in religious terms is the woman who has had an extra-marital affair, receives forgiveness and acceptance from both her husband and the sacraments of the Church: she is happy for a while but later on becomes frigid and unable to enjoy her sexual relationship with her husband. She feels unworthy. Because this false guilt links back to a real guilt, it all gets very confusing!

An added difficulty is that both psychiatrists and religious preachers point in different ways to the reality that many people fail to develop a sense of moral responsibility or do so in a haphazard way that brings them immense confusion and pain and results in apparently immoral behaviour. In his book *Basic Types of Pastoral Counselling*, Howard J. Clinebell sees this as the area where 'confrontational counselling is appropriate' as helping people to distinguish right and wrong, but goes on before the end of the relevant chapter to qualify what he means by a confrontational counselling which is appropriate both from the point of view of the psychiatrist and the Christian.[7] He quotes James A. Knight: 'Pastors and teachers have not always understood the meaning of confrontation in counselling. It is often confused with a vertical type of authoritarianism, moralistic preachments, or hostile attacks indulged in under the guise of righteous indignation.' His advice is that the method should be used with restraint, that its success depends on the maturity of the priest or helper using it and that the emphasis should be on helping the person come to reality (self confrontation) in his or her own time and in his or her own way.

This makes me feel that it would be wiser not to speak at all of confrontational counselling but rather to talk of the element of confrontation which should enter at the appropriate moment into all Christian counselling but never become an end in itself. This is particularly true as we try to move away from the residual tendencies to put priest or minister on a pedestal ('he's God's

17

mouthpiece' or 'he's studied it all for years' or 'he leads such a holy—separate?—life'), which combines with the enthusiasm of the man 'burning to change the world for the better' to produce a rather dangerous cocktail of telling people what's right and wrong, and people abdicating any personal development of responsibility for their own lives and decisions.

The complications of trying to determine whether the guilt a person is experiencing is appropriate or an emotional reaction to pain means that a priest/minister must listen for a long time before enabling the person to present their sin to Christ for forgiveness. The guilt involved in the grieving process has already been mentioned. It is now well established that the most tragic result of rape or sexual abuse, especially when it is incestuous, is a desperate feeling of guilt in the victim which ranges across all the person's life and relationships. They feel particularly responsible for having caused the destructive anger they perceive in the person abusing them, and if the case emerges into the light of day and the abuser is brought to justice the guilt is even more difficult to deal with. The battered wife or husband, the married person who is consistently undermined by criticism, sarcasm or scape-goating ends by being convinced of his/her own uselessness and guilt. The last thing any of them need is being confronted with their guilt or even having 'forgiveness' offered for their guilt. Both would and often do reinforce the damage that has already been done to them.

B) *The Christian View of Guilt Clarified*

A study of the Christian teaching and practice of forgiveness goes a long way to reinforce the central insight of modern counselling philosophy that real objective freely incurred guilt is much less common than often presumed. This is all the more remarkable since sin and guilt are at the heart of the Christian message and, as Dr Grossouw observes, 'Where the notion of sin is lost, as it is to a great extent in the modern world, Christianity may be compared to a clanging bell in a deserted village.'[8] Though this is undoubtedly true, confusion with false guilt obscures real guilt and likewise prevents false guilt being healed.

The full notion of sin is the end result of the whole path of God's revelation and to understand the concept as it developed is the best possible way to clarify when real guilt occurs. It begins with the pre-biblical rather awed and fearful perception by man that there are certain limitations on human existence which it is dangerous to over-step: trangressions against these covered the breaking of taboos and laws of nature as well as moral transgressions. To this the Bible immediately adds the dimension of sin as a revolt against the Creator who is due the full service of man. Next comes the covenant idea which presents sin as breaking the personal relationship first of all between God and the whole Jewish people and then latterly between God and the individual Jew.

The prophets appear at times to be black pessimists as they preach untiringly about the sinfulness of man, the twistedness of man (as the commonest word implies), but they are the ones who build up the sense of the holiness of God (for example Jeremiah's horror 'Depart from me O God for I am a man of sinful lips' and Ezechiel's opening vision of the majesty and remoteness of the glory of God). This holiness of God is then balanced by their picture of a patient God waiting for the return of his people, the return of the sinner. 'Even if your sins are like scarlet, I will make you as white as snow.'

Both the Old Testament and the New Testament point to a view of sin which stands out in marked contrast to all non-Christian views. As the Dutch Catechism put it:

> The Christian revelation . . . says that the great guilt of man is not ultimately the fact that a cog-wheel is in the wrong place (as Marxism holds) but that his will is freely set on evil. It says again that evil is not ultimately just the imperfection of a free creature, which can be corrected by intelligence and energy (as Buddhism in inclined to hold) but man's turning away from God, which cannot be set right by man. Then, the ultimate wickedness is not the transgression of a cold, lofty law (as Islam generally holds) but an offence against personal love. Finally, it is not just an offence against man (as humanism holds) but also an offence against our creator and redeemer.[9]

Sin is presented by Hosea as an offence against God seen as our lover, a lover who is prepared to pay off those who have enslaved the loved one in a net of guilt and extortion (Hos. 1–3). Jesus then goes on to speak of sin as an offence against a loving Father who comes more than half way down the road to welcome back the prodigal son and is prepared to celebrate his return in a way that transforms all niggardly human standards of forgiveness and reconciliation. (Lk. 15:11–24). Sin is the power that in the Old Testament is pictured in the destructive power of the flood (material creation) and the tower of Babel (personal relationships) and is almost personified in Pauline theology as the power which dominates and enslaves man without God and brings all the sufferings of sin which work in us to bring death (see Rom. 6 and 7). The flesh (*sarx*) is that combination of the weakness of human nature and being born into a world where sin exists and where one person's sin provokes sin in the other, even or especially in the precious but frail relationship of parent and child. Such is that 'original sin' which means we all need God's forgiving and transforming power in Baptism . . . and in the sacrament of Reconciliation (binding and loosing, forgiving and retaining) in our continuing struggle after Baptism. This Anna Blaman puts very well in a fine message quoted again in the Dutch Catechism:

> I realised that it was simply impossible for a human being to be, and remain 'good' or 'pure'. If for instance, I wanted to be attentive in one direction, it could only be at the cost of neglecting another. If I gave my heart to one thing, I left another in the cold—I came up against my human short-comings again and again. If I could only tell myself 'Well you are no saint, so you might as well be content with yourself the way you are'. But it would not help, because I am not content and so . . . my human shortcomings are also my human guilt— a guilt which sometimes shows itself all too clearly in the consequences of what we have done, or left undone.

This whole picture of sin emphasises that in the middle of our human frailty sin only occurs when we knowingly choose to be selfish and self-centred rather than respond to the love of God living in our hearts. Yet we must be like the publican saying 'Lord have mercy on me a sinner' rather than the self-congratulatory Pharisee. The one we meet with our prayer is, however, the one who said to the adulterous woman 'Has no one condemned you? . . . neither do I condemn you . . . go away and don't sin any more.' The silence which intervened points us back to the listening silence of counselling. From it arise shared insights rather than imposed solutions or solutions which no-one is really able to listen to.

When we turn to the post-Vatican 11 developments in the sacrament of Reconciliation in the Roman Catholic Church, the notion of repentance has moved clearly away from any confusion with mere regret (which may or may not be there without damaging the sincerity of the repentance) or shame (which may be founded or unfounded without affecting the repentance). Repentance has gone back to its origins in *shuv* in the Hebrew and *metanoia* in the Greek to emphasise that turning away from sin involves a very real conversion, a turning one's life upside down and inside out. Rather than being expected to produce a neat list of habitual delicts, the penitent is invited in the context of a more relaxed encounter with Our Lord to express what he/she knows or feels to be disjointed in his/her life. This individual encounter will have been prepared for and followed up by communal reflection. In this setting the authoritative word of forgiveness becomes incarnate in a way that respects the mystery of our perception of when we can truly be said to be humanly guilty and our need to open ourselves to God's goodness even though still 'seen as it were in a glass darkly'.

A parallel movement exists within the Protestant Churches. To return to Clinebell again: 'Inescapably, the minister is a symbol of the values of his community and tradition. Many people come to him for help precisely because they feel guilty, often without being consciously aware of it.' Later, he describes extended counselling with a man who had done irreparable damage to someone else: the minister concluded the counselling with a session in his pulpit robes at the Communion railing. He invited the man to pray for an awareness of God's forgiveness, followed this with a prayer of absolution and concluded it with the Our Father.

In both situations we find the process of coming to forgiveness and reconciliation being extended into a longer process because of the theological reflection which has taken place about the nature of the unfolding of human guilt as a necessary preliminary to the essentially religious experience.

There is perhaps no other area of human concern which demands more attention to what Paul Tillich calls the principle of mutuality (a mutual sharing between helper and helped) and yet on the surface it would seem the area in which it does not arise at all. Forgiveness of real guilt, or the developing of a sense of guilt about the areas where we are unaware of our faults, or the separation out of the areas of neurotic guilt, must all stop being given 'from above'. As the Letter to the Hebrews says: ' . . . it is not as if we had a high priest who was incapable of feeling our weakness with us; but we have one who has been tempted in every way that we are, though he is without sin.' (Heb. 4:15)

In this light Tillich's words ring out: 'The pastoral counsellor must participate in the situation of the person needing care. This participation expresses itself not only in words of acceptance, but also in ways of communicating to the counselee the fact that the counselor was and is in the same situation.' The road is then open for the guilty person to be freed from false guilt, to be confronted with the reality of real guilt and be enabled to meet the forgiving God who helps us to ask for forgiveness, change what has to be turned upside down and begin to live a new life. The forgiveness comes from above: the road to that forgiveness must follow the pattern of all human paths of development and personal change.

C) Conclusion

The conclusion of an American study of guilt is a salutary warning for Christian pastors approaching what are perceived as intense feelings of guilt and being tempted to leap in with words of forgiveness or calls to repentance before listening first. 'Guilt implies an offence against God, neighbour or self and can usually be alleviated by cessation of the offence and/or reparation. When such a change takes place, there is no need for guilt feelings. The feelings frequently labelled guilt feelings, usually long lasting and pervasive, are really indications that the persons believe themselves inferior. If we can laugh at ourselves—or at least smile inwardly—we can objectify the dynamics, see more clearly what they achieve for us, and so lessen or eliminate them.' (Joseph L. Hart)[10] The priest or minister should be much less ready to offer palliative words of forgiveness, for palliatives reinforce feelings of guilt and do not remove them.

Love, Loneliness and 'Loving too Much'

In his book *Why am I afraid to love?* John Powell points out that 'although it is difficult to accept, the psychological scars that we have acquired during our first seven years remain in some way with us for life. We are, each of us, the product of those who have loved us ... or refused to love us' or loved us in a disturbed way.[11] Christian theology and modern psychology agree in emphasising that no-one can love unless they are first loved. St John emphasises that the love he writes about so beautifully is not so much our love for God but his love for us. (1 Jn. 4) That love makes all else possible, but our ability to love is quite literally handicapped by not experiencing the physical and personally tangible love of God as reflected in other human beings. This must make the Christian care-er hesitate before speaking glibly of God's love to reassure or comfort those who are hurt and damaged. To speak to a class of children about God as our loving Father when the only father many of them know is a drunk or a wife-batterer or a child-abuser is a well-known but extraordinarily dangerous exercise. Similarly, to preach unthinkingly about the 'glorious love of a good Christian family' is not to have sat for hours counselling those with problems within marriage. In the majority of Western countries today one third of the congregations in the churches will be divorced or separated, one third will be experiencing major problems and only one third will be in any position to hear the message of the preacher.

In a book written to mark the twenty-first anniversary of the Carr-Gomm Society (which provides homes for lonely people) Christopher Martin speaks rightly of loneliness as the leprosy of the day. It affects the young, the old, the middle-aged, the bereaved, the healthy and the victims of AIDS alike; it affects the divorced—and in a very tragic way it exists within many marriages. He quotes Ron in his mid-twenties 'I feel so lonely, I could scream. When I stand up, when I sit down, when I turn around, I cannot bear to be inside my skin.'[12] That's what I mean by being lonely.

The Christian Church should of course be the antidote to such loneliness, not only with its faith that God the Father, Son and Holy Spirit come and make their home in us when we respond to their love but also because we are all called to be members of one family. As Paul made clear, in Christ there is neither Jew nor Greek, male nor female ... we are all one in Christ Jesus. (Gal. 3:28) We should bear one another's burdens as members of one family. Yet once again how that Church community is realised is crucial.

23

Christopher Martin speaks of the isolating shock when a lonely person goes to a Christian retreat house to be faced with a neon sign 'Jesus loves you—no smoking'. In place of such an attitude he quotes with great wisdom the famous picture of Holman Hunt which hangs in St Paul's Cathedral in London: 'Behold I stand at the door and knock' is the caption, but the door has no doorhandle and there are thorns up around the doorpost. The figure of Christ with his lantern patiently waits. That sort of waiting is the antithesis of many clumsy visits by Church 'neighbourhood groups' to the old and particularly to the bereaved. Thrusting ourselves into other people's loneliness only serves at times to increase that loneliness. Many people are so hurt inside that coping with unsolicited visits is almost more than they can handle, especially when the visitors insist on speaking words of comfort.

At the end of the day, the Christian has the answer to the destructive evil of loneliness in our society, but the patience of being available and listening for the invitation to come in is the skill of Christian counselling. It opens the door to a new world where loneliness is often healed by a combination of caring presence and respect for the other person's solitude. We need to have the space to be alone but the knowledge of the closeness of the love of others to sustain us in that love. The Dean of Salisbury Cathedral on 12 October 1980 put it this way: 'A wise writer once said that husband and wife should be guardians of each other's solitude. Certainly, parents should guard the solitude of their children. For to respect and guard our own solitude is to acknowledge our individual uniqueness and the unique growth we each must achieve.' He quoted Vita Sackville West about the 'power of being alone' and how the high point of this power is the quiet prayer which allows us to hear God in the quietness of our hearts.

The most frightening of the areas of loneliness in our society is the loneliness of young people and the rising toll of suicide among them makes that clear. One very practical response was the book *Is anyone there?* edited by Monica Dickens and Rosemary Sutcliff.[13] In it a group of writers used their skill to convey to young people that 'someone out there feels the same way as you do'. Col is so bored and frustrated that he can only feel hate and guilt; Mark and Casey fall in love on holiday but have to fly home to opposite corners of the world; and there is fifteen year old Tommy who's lonely but too shy to dance. For all of them, there is a lesson for the Christian care-er: and perhaps it is close to the new ideas of a theology of story, that we must tell the story of our own journey—and Christ's journey—through uncertainties, before young people can begin to listen. And first, we must listen to their story—as it is, not as we would like it to be.

'Loving too much' seems to be the antithesis of Christianity and yet Christ's command of love had the possibility built in. We are to love one another as *we love ourselves* for the sake of God. Modern child psychology underlines the fact that we cannot love one another unless we first love ourselves. Yet self-love is described as a sin in the old books of spirituality. What they are really talking about is self-centredness, self-absorption, but it so easily became a spirituality of hating self or putting one's own self to death to become alive to Christ or to allow Christ to take over. John Powell's writings have done much to counter this attitude but more needs to be done. This becomes critical when religious attitudes have reinforced the self-hate which is one of the most damaging effects of child-battering, child sexual abuse, rape, wife battering and mental cruelty within marriage.

At this point, Robin Norwood's writings are extremely helpful, especially her classic text *Women who love too much*[14] which would be better entitled 'People who love too much'. These are the people for whom loving other people becomes almost unbelievably an unhealthy addiction. Robin Norwood suggests that if being in love means being in pain, the person is suffering from an unhealthy pattern of behaviour which has developed as a response to the problems of childhood. She speaks of people for whom having somebody to love is the most important thing in life in the sense of over-riding every other rational consideration. Another symptom is a constant driving restlessness, a belief that with 'the right man or woman' the person involved would no longer feel depressed or lonely. It's interesting that she comes to the conclusion that developing a spirituality is a critical tool for the recovery from self-destructiveness that 'loving too much' brings. She defines this spirituality as 'letting go of self-will, of the determination to make things happen the way you think they should'. It means accepting you don't know what's best for yourself or the other person in a given situation, considering

25

other solutions and outcomes, being willing to hold still, be open and wait for guidance for yourself. It means letting go of all fear (all the 'what ifs?') and despair (all the 'if onlys').

This letting go of self-will and accepting that we don't know what's best for ourselves and others seems to me to fit in remarkably well with the 'Thy will be done, not mine' of the Our Father and the picture of Christ in the Letter to the Hebrews 'Lo, I have come to do thy will, O God' (Heb. 10:7). It also fits in with Fr Jock Dalrymple's emphasis on the development of prayer from the 'wordy'—telling God a great list of what we think he should do—to the prayer of silence and listening.[15] If all this is so, the Christian care-er is called to facilitate the development of that listening sort of prayer which allows changed attitudes to emerge from the pain and loneliness of the one who prays.

To urge someone who loves too much that all we need do is imitate Christ's unselfish love is to destroy the person on the rocks of his/her own addiction to caring and to ensure that such as the dependent alcoholic, gambler, drug addict or self-centred insecure spouse never has the chance to grow into real love. To suggest to them to go to God in prayer for the strength to keep caring and loving is to reinforce feelings of guilt, failure and loneliness rather than heal them. We must encourage people to listen to their own needs, to open those needs to new answers in prayer; and we must help them listen to a God who may well be encouraging them to look after themselves so that they can love others in a way which will allow them in turn to make efforts for themselves and to change for the better.

Suicide

One of the most tragic and challenging characters in the whole of the new Testament is Judas. The musical *Jesus Christ Superstar* capitalised on the complex picture given of his motivation in the gospels and ended by making him almost the hero of the whole dramatic presentation. On the other hand, Christian tradition from the New Testament onwards gives the picture of a man corrupted by the money he administered and by the subtle arguments of the Pharisees. After the betrayal and crucifixion went through, Judas was so consumed with both real guilt and what we would recognise today as false guilt—the shame, the conviction that no-one could ever forgive him, the reinforcement of being a failure—that he hanged himself. In many ways, Peter—the leader of the group—failed just as badly by denying Christ not just once but three times, despite his boasting that he could never do such a thing. Peter, however, was also a victim of confused motivation and one look from Jesus was enough for him not just to realise his guilt but to remember that Jesus says God will forgive not just seven times but 'seventy times seven'.

The difference between Peter and Judas is not as was once thought the difference between good and bad but rather the 'x' factor that precipitates suicide in one person with a problem and a background of damage and in another produces heroic perseverance and courage, often in a coded way. The problem, however, would seem to be not so much that those who commit suicide don't tell us of their inability to overcome being damaged and be healed, but rather that they tell us but we do not hear what they are saying—until it is too late.

Hovering over the whole area of the Church's care towards those who are thinking of suicide or have attempted it is the attitude built into popular mythology that this is the worst sin of all. Typical of this is the caller to the radio counselling programme or the Samaritans who asks very simply 'Will God send me to hell for all eternity if I commit suicide?' On being reassured that a loving God would not throw such a distressed person as the caller into hell, the answer can immediately come back 'That's fine then. I'm leaving you now to commit suicide because I just can't go on any longer.'

Canon Law used to legislate clearly for the denial of a Church funeral and the burial in unconsecrated ground of those who killed themselves. That has stuck in the popular mind even though the present position of Canon 1184 allows for much more flexible pastoral judgment. Church funeral rites are to be denied 'unless they gave some signs of repentance before death' to 'manifest sinners to whom a Church funeral could not be granted without public scandal to the faithful'. Fortunately, public understanding of those who commit suicide has grown to the extent that it is hard to imagine public scandal to the faithful at least in countries like Britain.[16]

It could be argued that the popular conception of suicide as putting one outside God's love and forgiveness increases the likelihood of suicide because it increases the self-hatred and depression which is a major contributory factor in a suicide decision. Clearly the negative threat of suicide being the ultimate sin, since it destroys our God-given life and usurps his dominion, can in theory prevent suicide by making the sin more clear; but the general conviction today is that a sensitive listening community which witnesses to the value of even the most seemingly valueless life is a much more powerful factor. The gentle Jesus who could speak of God's care for every sparrow or of the beauty of the fields which is here today and gone tomorrow, and the forgiving God who comes more than half way down the road to welcome back any human being no matter how worthless he/she feels, must surely be incarnated into our Churches to give hope to the dramatically rising number of those who are suicidal in our society.

Reactions among Christian care-ers to threats of suicide vary from the dismissive—those that threaten it never do it (even though seventy per cent who actually commit suicide have talked about it in some way in the previous three months and nobody very much had listened)—to those who threaten their own stability by getting so involved with the suicidal that their eventual death makes them feel a total failure both as human beings and as Christians (even though advice and counselling in themselves are acknowledged to be incapable of deterring someone who is determined to commit suicide).

Eugene Kennedy in *On Becoming a Counsellor* gives a fairly well accepted identikit of the individual most likely to commit suicide: 'the depressed man over forty years of age, single, divorced, or without close friends in his life; persons who live alone; alcoholics, of whom twenty per cent die by their own hands; persons who have recently suffered a great loss; or older people who are physically ill.'[17] The sad thing, however, is that it can happen to anyone in certain circumstances and that the figures for young people committing suicide or attempting it seriously have screamed to massive proportions.

Women attempt suicide four times oftener than men, but men complete suicide four times oftener than women. Both sexes, however, come to consider suicide 'when they can no longer cope' and so this apparently common sense description serves as a flashing amber light which should never be ignored until the possibility of suicide has been looked at sensitively. There are many books which describe the full range of warning signs; they repay careful study for they illustrate very clearly that advising somebody to take their troubles to God in prayer is to miss the whole point. George Engel gives a useful list:

(a) 'giving up' feelings of helplessness or hopelessness;
(b) a depreciated picture of oneself;
(c) a loss of satisfaction from personal relationships or from one's role in life;
(d) a break in one's sense of continuity between the past, present and future;
(e) a reactivation of memories of earlier periods of 'giving up' on life.[18]

Bernard Steinzer is more graphic: 'he who takes his life has given up all hope of the possibility of affection ... I hear suicidal thoughts and the cries for help before the final spasm of despair takes over.'[19]

The leaflets published by The Samaritans provide the same message in simple terms, backed up by the frightening statistics. In the face of all this the hard work for the Christian community is to make those on the fringes of life feel that affection which enables the disintegrating human being to feel the sense of belonging and acceptance which can alone bring hope. It's a matter of making tangible Christ's words of healing, reconciliation and respect for the person being all he/she can be. 'By this love you have for one another, everyone will know that you are my disciples.' (Jn. 13:35). Creating that atmosphere of warm caring and non-intrusive love will not persuade every potential suicide that there is hope but it will heal many broken hearts. Allied with this must be a response to what St Paul invited us to do, 'to bear one another's burdens'. Dr Paul Pretzel says we must take immensely seriously any threat to commit suicide. This does not of course mean over-reacting in a way which would destroy any further confiding by the despairing, but it particularly means that when a person threatening suicide is clear about

(1) specific means
(2) lethal means
(3) available means,

then the likelihood of suicide is very great.[20]

One last point to be considered: even if we are convinced as Christians that suicide is wrong and contradicts the sacredness

29

of life, have we any right not to respect the decision of someone who decided either that they could do nothing else or that this was the most unselfish thing they could do for others? The people of Holland have even begun to tolerate euthanasia for the terminally ill and ten thousand each year (eight per cent of those who die) now choose euthanasia. Two thirds of the doctors cooperate.

Be that as it may, what perhaps we could agree about more easily is that whatever we say before the event, the Christian care-er must be able to accept and reassure the attempted suicide on the way to recovery, and must be able to work with the bereaved in a suicide case with a clear vision of how little blame can be apportioned to the person who acts so tragically and so irreversibly at that point when all other options seem to the person to have disappeared. Only when the counsellor grasps that mystery with reverence, in acknowledgment of human frailty and the space the indwelling Spirit allows for human searching and human mistakes, can there be Christian caring both for the attempted suicide and the bereaved who are left with all the conflicting emotions which follow on that ultimate act of despair.

Rape, Spouse Battering, Physical and Sexual Abuse of Children
The general heading of domestic violence raises its own general questions for the preacher, the parish visitor, the confessor or the care-er. They are all characterised by a false guilt which the Christian minister will either reinforce or help to heal. The Catholic Church has a particular problem in this area which was highlighted by a retired American policeman, Harry J. O'Reilly, in a lecture in Teesside Polytechnic in 1981. He observed that boys had all sorts of role models among the saints to imitate but girls were presented with St Agnes, St Lucy and St Maria Goretti, all of whom died at the hands of rapists rather than give up their chastity. 'What a message' he said 'those good little Catholic girls are getting: it's better to die than get raped.' The advice he gave to his three Catholic daughters was straight to the point: 'Stay alive—rape is not a fate worse than death—death is worse than getting raped. Stay alive and we will help you put your life back together—we in the helping network, we in society, are going to help you to reintegrate your life. You don't have to die. You don't have to fight if you're not a good fighter. Fighting at the wrong time will get you killed.'

He spoke from a background of having stood in New York City over the bodies of more than 100 women who had tried to fight and who had been mainly strangled or had something like a hairbrush stuck down their throats to silence them. It was fascinating to read between the lines of his speech to hear how this policeman had evolved from feeling that he should be able to say 'it's right to struggle' or 'it's alright not to struggle' or 'it's better not to struggle' to a position where he concludes: 'I have learned to say to the victim, "You did the right thing because you are here to talk about it".' This led him to emphasise to his officers what he sees as the critical importance of what the first copper says to the victim.

Even more critical for any victim with religious convictions will be what the first 'religious person' gives as their first reaction. The classic situation is illustrated by the victim of a gang rape who had planned to offer her virginity as a wedding gift: 'I know I should be a Christian and forgive them . . . but it was so important to me. Then I feel guilty about how I feel.' Similar is the reaction of the victim of sustained incestuous rape who sobs that no-one could ever marry her because she is so dirty.

The roots of such emotions are not just psychological. They lie deep in the aberrations of Christian theology and I believe these must be explored at some length if we are to set aside the barriers which will otherwise prevent Christian counselling being effective. It is a long and winding story.

About the time of St Augustine, Greek thought became in Christianity the re-interpreter of ideas which originally existed in quite different Semitic categories of thought and definition. Whereas the 'spirit' (*pneuma*) in St Paul indicated the person living in union with Christ and the 'flesh' (*sarx*) meant the whole human being living without Christ, the new interpretation was to see the spirit as good as the body as evil or at least so profoundly imperfect that it could not be the object of sacraments like the sacrament of the sick and the sacrament of marriage. From this St Augustine went so far as to conclude that sex in marriage could only be justified because of the 'higher goods' such as having children.

From then on, the beautiful biblical insights of man and woman in their togetherness making up the image of God, and the dramatic use in the Song of Songs of sex as the embodiment and illustrative reflection of God's love, were lost sight of almost completely. We even had the spectre of medieval monks and nuns wrestling with sexual temptation (often imagining the devil in the process) and engaging in masochistic self-flagellation in the belief that they were doing penance for their sins, whereas modern psychology makes plain they were in fact becoming more sexually disturbed in the process.

What has to be restored is the full Old and New Testament appreciation of sex as the normal embodiment of God's love. Even in the context of prostitution, St Paul is able in 1 Cor. 6:12–20 to make it clear that for him—despite the unfounded condemnations of him as a hater of women and sex—the sexual union within marriage is not a marginal erotic function but an act which by its very nature so absorbs and expresses the whole personality as to be an entirely unique kind of self-revelation and commitment. Then the parallel in Eph. 5:21–33 of Christian husband and wife, Adam and Eve, and Christ and the Church brings back the Genesis teaching of the complementariness of man and woman mirroring in their married love the inner reality of God himself.

Both texts taken together bring St Paul very close to modern insights such as those of A. Watt in *Nature, Man and Woman* where sexuality is described as 'pervading every human relationship but assuming a particular intensity at certain points'.[21] Alistair V. Campbell in *Rediscovering Pastoral Care* is even clearer: 'The radiance of sexuality consists in the pleasurable awareness of possessing a body which is neither male nor female and the joyful recognition of the maleness and femaleness of others. It is graceful when it coheres in the life of the individual possessing it, when it enhances the quality of all his relationships.'[22] The second Vatican Council itself made it clear that married people don't become saints by the extras they do but through their marriage. Marriage is a saving state in which the partners are enabled to achieve their appropriate Christian perfection: it is defined as a personal community within which the partners give and accept each other.[23]

Such a picture is a long way from Luther seeing marriage as a 'hospital for incurables, which prevents its inmates from falling into graver sin'[24]. Again too it seems light years away from the attitudes described by Henri Gheon in writing of the parents of

32

St Therese of Lisieux, remarking that their 'marriage bed was sacred to a married love that sought to be nothing but a duty'.[25] The effect on St Therese was that she always felt uncomfortable in her body. Perhaps the most dramatic contrast of realities comes when preachers condemn 'bad thoughts' in young people in the face of research which shows that young men between sixteen and twenty-six think of sex every other minute. Until a radical new theology of the goodness of sex becomes commonplace, there will be almost insurmountable extra problems in coping with the damage done to people by sexual aberrations.

For Catholics the spirituality which emphasises Mary's virginity rather than her motherhood brings added problems for young girls and particularly for those who are the victims of sexual attacks. When purity is presented as such a shining ideal, then not only sexual sin but also any sexual attack only too easily reinforces the feelings of being dirty which invade the victim of the sexual assault. All this demands a sensitivity from the priest or minister in counselling any people with religious faith when they are the victims of sexual attack.

Even more critical than this, however, is the factor which is common to all assaults, sexual or otherwise—and particularly to the physical and sexual abuse of children. Jacqueline Spring, in her book *Cry Hard and Swim*, speaks vividly of her feelings as an incest survivor. She likens herself to a concentration camp victim:

> When I read about those camps, and survivors' accounts of what they were like, I realise with a shock that, on some level that is not physical, I have been there. I know about the self-effacement, the secret fantasies of what it would be like not to be small, trivial, powerless, hungry for love. I know about how vital, but how dangerous these fantasies were . . . And most of all I know about the guilt of it, the strange phenomenon by which the survivors come to accept the situation as normal, to forget any other way of life, to be so ashamed of being human in this animal squalor, that they pretend even to themselves that they are being correctly treated, because they are animals, disobedient, untrustworthy animals.[26]

She goes on to speak of 'the habit of shouldering the blame which is well-developed in the abused child. The alternative, to admit the parent's guilt, is almost harder to bear.' As a result 'the

33

inner fences, the most jagged wires of all, seal off the clear memory of the pain and humiliation.' It is those inner fences that the Christian care-er has to be aware of.

When we come to consider how a return to normality can be achieved for those who are the victims of violence, we have to move into the area of helping the victims to overcome the inner fences to begin the process of mourning the loss of the many things which have been ripped away—the process which has already been described with regard to bereavement. Even more so than with bereavement, the process can have five or five hundred stages (M.A. Simpson *The Facts of Death*) and each represents a hurdle which the care-er must try to identify and be sensitive to.[27]

Shock very often prevents a victim taking in what has happened and so there can be a long gap between the attack and the moment when the anaesthetic finally wears off and the pain is unbearable. Denial is the phenomenon where the victim mentally accepts the trauma and dismisses it as not important. Life must go on. The danger is that those around may either accept this or even use it themselves to avoid their own sympathetic pain. With anger, it's surely not wrong to say people should be angry, when Christ could be angry in the temple and when so many psalms provide such a helpful vehicle for such anger in prayer. More subtly damaging is the anger that turns inwards causing depression or outwards against helpers—or the anger that says to the victim that they should have been able to do something to prevent the attack. Particularly guilty of this are the mothers of sons who beat up their wives and most tragically the wives who say to their children that they should surely have been able to do something to stop the husband's sexual advances. Anxiety and depression are more intractable consequences of violence, but helping the victim to mourn will always have a healing role. 'Happy are those who mourn' may not be just a proclamation of faith that Christ can overcome the worst of mourning and that our helplessness and our turning to him can finally bring deep peace—it may also be a reminder of the healing that can only come when the Christian care-er is prepared to give time and space for the person to mourn properly all that has been so cruelly ripped away.

One of the clearest examples of the dangers and opportunities for Christian caring in this area is the Satanic ritual abuse of children. The examples I have dealt with concerned one or both of the parents of the child along with uncles and aunts but Maureen Davies, director of a Christian organisation *Reachout Trust*, has pointed out in a study paper (in 1989) that children can be recruited by means of drugs, pornography, ouija boards, occult magazines, blackmail by pictures taken of what happened at drink/drug parties: and at railway stations when the young people have run away from home. The catalogue of abuse is almost beyond belief. The children are urinated on: and urine, excrement, semen and blood are smeared all over their bodies. They are made to eat the mixture and drink the blood. They are placed in coffins, cages and cupboards. They are tied up and subjected to perverted sex from adults with additional torture by the insertion of instruments. They are forced to have sex with living and dead animals and made to eat beetles. Snakes are allowed to roam over the children. Worst of all is the fact that women they call 'brood mares' are forced to be pregnant: the child is aborted live at five and a half months. The blood is drunk.

It all sounds incredible. When I first came across it from a girl who gradually unfolded the story, I presumed for a long time that a great deal of it was the result of deep pain and as such a defensive product of her imagination, but I kept listening. With two such girls, however, the clinical psychologists to whom I was able to refer them confirmed the reality of what had happened to these girls, by matching their experiences in circumstances, time and place to those of other victims of the same Satanic circle who had come from quite different routes to their attention. One of these was in the Lowlands and one in the Highlands of Scotland.

These episodes reinforced in me the conviction that as Christian ministers, we must listen and listen and listen even when what we are hearing seems utterly beyond credibility.

The religious questions which followed on were quite challenging. I do not believe that traditional Church exorcism of the devil is at all appropriate, because I believe it reinforces the fear which keeps the persons enslaved, the fear that they are—because of sin, sex and excrement—unclean (and need to be cleansed) and the fear that the devil has enslaving power. Fundamentalist Christians would point to the exorcisms of the New Testament but modern scripture studies would suggest that these were not so much rituals as rather a proclamation that Christ's power could overcome and heal everything that was feared and not understood. Mental illness came into this category. The devil symbolised all the power of evil outside Christ, material as well as moral. The proper ritual then for me, and the one I have found most effective, is the normal ritual of Church life which points quietly and reassuringly to the sacraments as meetings with the Christ who has already overcome all the power of evil. In him and so in us, the devil has no power. There is no need of an extra elaborate ritual, which would focus fear, to destroy what in Christian faith is already made ineffectual by Christ's Resurrection.

A pastor speaking too quickly will block the suffering young person's ability to speak of Satanic ritual abuse; listening will slowly set the person free to speak. Speaking the wrong words, the words of misunderstood symbolism in the Bible, can reinforce the false guilt and fear. In both cases I speak of, a fundamentalist Christian group made the problem much worse by the well-meaning 'casting out of the devil'. In both cases, being enabled to listen to Jesus' words of reassurance helped to set them free. This freedom enabled them to separate out the feelings of uncleanness, guilt and 'being different' from any idea that this indicates possession by the devil; once separated out, these feelings could be seen to be emotional defence mechanisms against the hurt and shame which had been inflicted.

Drink and Drugs

Those for whom drink or drugs are a problem and those suffering from AIDS or from being diagnosed as HIV positive, are all linked by the extreme reactions they are capable of provoking in Christian care-ers. One extreme is that of those who see drink, drugs and AIDS as the realm of the devil—everything from the 'demon drink' to seeing AIDS as the judgment of God on society. The other extreme is that of the care-er who allows himself or herself to be manipulated by the person with the problem. It's only too well known that those who cover up for the addict perpetuate the problem, put off the day when the addict will sink low enough to realise that he/she needs to ask for help, and as a result can play their part in destroying the very person whom they love and want to protect with what is often saint-like devotion and martyrdom. We dare not underestimate the courage and generous faithfulness of such care-ers, but we must gently nudge them to a new perspective both for their own sake and for the sake of the person trapped by the substance abused.

Ever since St Paul suggested that while drunkenness was always well to the fore in his list of sins, but that nonetheless it was a good thing for us to 'take a cup of wine for our stomach's sake', the Church's position has been ambivalent. Jesus himself was criticised because he and his disciples drank (you can almost hear the pejorative connotations in that word) while John the Baptist and his disciples did not. The monks and friars in medieval times were—from Chaucer on—slated for over-indulgence. The post-Reformation ministers (Dr Bonum Magnum in Scotland was a striking example) came to be accused in similar vein. Each time the Earl of Huntley converted to Protestantism (several times!), he and the whole of Aberdeen Kirk Session got drunk together.

Alongside these very visible happenings, there were ascetic movements in both Roman Catholicism and Protestantism which eschewed alcohol altogether and, in the nineteenth century, the total abstinence movement in the whole of the British Isles was about the only factor which drew enthusiasts from every Christian tradition—and this campaign was extended into the area of indulgence with drugs. These enthusiasts—as in the normal paradox—dramatically increased the circle of guilt for the heavy drinker or drug abuser, and so could be accused of making the problem worse.[28] Fiery preaching that drink and drugs take us into slavery to the devil reinforced the guilt and self-hatred which are quickly taken to characterise the over-indulgent and lead them to feel they are evil and that there is no possibility of improvement for them. The challenge for the Christian care-er is to allow the drink or drug-abused to find again their surviving God-given dignity and thus find the motivation and hope which alone can sustain them on a journey out of dependency.

Some of the commonly used approaches to helping those who over-indulge can illustrate the ramifications of the Christian challenge. If alcoholism or drug addiction is an illness, Christ's ministry to the sick comes into play—and so does the Church's sacrament of the sick or laying on of the hands. *Alcoholics Anonymous* and *Narcotics Anonymous* arise from that conviction, but they have broad areas of agreement with the critics who deny the illness concept in maintaining that while people are not responsible for their illness they are one hundred per cent responsible for their recovery. The historian of AA, Dr Ernest Kurtz, believes their remarkable success is based on 'the shared honesty of mutual vulnerability, openly acknowledged'. Critics, however, feel that the twelve steps to recovery, with their references to 'a power greater than themselves' and 'prayer and meditation to improve a conscious contact with God' makes AA and NA helpful for many but unhelpful and guilt-reinforcing for others. These critics would advocate intense individual or group counselling. For these reasons, the Christian advice must draw back from always advocating the approaches which seem to be 'more religious'.

Another approach to be kept in mind is called the Minnesota Model. It developed from that of AA and NA and involves people staying at a treatment centre for several weeks or going there after work. They are encouraged to admit their addiction, make a searching moral inventory of damage to themselves and others, renounce drink or other drugs, try to make amends and follow a treatment plan with this, usually including group discussions which help to reinforce abstinence.

The third approach is common to organisations like 'Lothian Council on Alcohol' (in Scotland) and books like the psychologist Dorothy Rowe's latest in which she says 'Alcoholism is a word we use to refer to something we choose to do in order to make ourselves feel better and try to blot out pain and fear.'[29] The response asked of counsellors is the Accept method, which is basically non-judgmental counselling. For some victims this counselling will have to take place in a protected environment where their other mental, physical and social problems can be taken care of, but the opinion is growing that more and more can be helped by patiently encouraging them to take responsibility for their own drinking. This method, however, is designedly not for those it calls 'alcohol addicts' i.e. someone who drinks large amounts of alcohol and suffers from withdrawal symptoms when he or she tries to stop drinking. The difference from AA is that they believe that everyone with alcohol problems should cut it out totally. Those using the approach of the Accept method believe that only some should do so:

(a) those who have suffered permanent medical damage already (a reminder that a referral to the doctor is essential for anyone with a drink problem);

(*b*) those who solved a previous drinking problem by drinking: they shouldn't start again;

(*c*) those who feel on balance that it's easier to stop altogether than to control what they drink;

(*d*) Pregnant women tempted by excessive drinking. (Here they are in line with recent research into 'foetal alcohol syndrome' which has established that more than 80g of pure alcohol per day—a quarter bottle of whisky—can cause mental deficiency, retard the growth of the foetus, affect its facial features and cause congenital anomalies. Professor Matthew Kaufmann of Edinburgh University believes that research even shows that alcohol can damage eggs before conception. Be that as it may, however, it is certain that 'foetal alcohol syndrome' is paralleled by the birth of heroin addicted children.)

These categories apart, most Health Education Groups believe that many others can be better helped by being taught to control alcohol, and consider that there is a higher possibility of success in these less extreme cases with this approach. For these less extreme cases, any religious stigma from a preached or counselled total abstinence line of thought can be harmful (as indeed in a different way with the alcohol-trapped victim). This finds its parallels with drug abuse when the pastor is faced with someone using soft drugs and maintaining that they are less harmful than drink. Is the Christian view that the moral response is to stop altogether? Or should the counsellor be non-judgmental and help the user of soft drugs to realise the legal problems (with blackmail often trapping the user into going further); the problems which arise from the personality becoming more passive and more easily manipulated; the sub-group-culture problems which again precipitate the user to the hard-drugs scene. As with alcohol, when true addiction is established, the Christian care-er must surely avoid reinforcing the purely negative self-hate by further condemnation and instead bring the combination of professional help, a new environment and Christian caring to re-establish that vision of new values of which the Christian ethic alone would be only a hollow echo.

Abstinence or control then is the Christian dilemma—at least with alcohol and with the use of prescribed drugs such as tranquillisers. Some would argue in favour of a legalised and controlled use of soft drugs but would retain a prohibition on the hard drugs which so rapidly destroy both personality and physical health by their self-absorbing craving and compulsion. There are difficult moral dilemmas in the schemes which try to combat self-perpetuating crime rings by making even hard drugs freely available to addicts in a controlled situation where they are at least given options of taking or not taking what will destroy them. Again too, it would be wrong to condemn those who give drugs or drug substitutes to dependents as part of the medical provision, in a society which does not give enough resources to provide for the person to person counselling which can perhaps alone wean an individual away from dependence. Until society and caring groups within and outside the Churches provide more of the pioneering counselling provision which exists in little pockets, condemnations from high moral stances will ring false.

Whatever approach is favoured, the consensus is clear that the addict will violently reject authoritarian advice or moral categorising. There is a strange combination in the addict of terrible honesty and an ingenious deviousness which result in the victims being unable to admit the truth to themselves. Listening for what and why is a long and frustrating process. Addicts all too often come from families where there was drug or alcohol abuse, sexual abuse, separation from parents or the loneliness of being children whose parents are obsessed by their own problems. Drugs or drink fill the gaping hole they experience within themselves. It is a major challenge for Christian caring.

AIDS

The phenomenon of 'AIDS' has reinforced the pastoral guidelines demanded by homosexuality (with its outcast syndrome), drink and drugs. All too often it has been described as God's punishment on homosexuals or on our corrupt society. To describe it in this way is to make God into a monster. In AIDS: Sharing the Pain, Bill Kirkpatrick agrees with Janet Morley that the Church has a moral obligation not to use the HIV infection to reclaim the age-old virtue of chastity, since this approach may well reinforce the negative and distorted aspects of Christian teaching, rather than redeeming what is positive and life enhancing. We should note that when chastity is produced as a solution to the threat of AIDS, we have shifted the meaning away from the area of moral choice and are describing behaviour that is simply prudent.'[30] Prudence may be a moral obligation but it should be kept quite separate from the presentation of ideals such as the fundamental one of sexual love being so good and so much God's gift that it should never be availed of in a context that is second best but kept instead for married commitment. Young people can respond to such an ideal even when they feel they might not always choose to live up to it—but they will see it as relevant and a challenge of Christ's love beckoning them onwards to the ideal.

Bill Kirkpatrick suggests that priests and ministers should be listening companions for those with AIDS, not turning the sufferer into a victim but into a friend as, together, they help each other to live with the infection—each recognising the other's sacredness. He quotes Peter Randall of 'Body Positive'—a London-based help group—to emphasise that what they need is space, where they're not confronted with attitudes of despair and hopelessness as they try to cope with the gradual disintegration of mind and body. 'Whatever you do to the least of my brothers' means that we have to serve Christ today in every victim of the disease.

Paul Clarke warns that 'The search for scapegoats is both pointless and potentially harmful, possibly more harmful than even the disease itself. Those who are bent on searching for scapegoats and who adopt dogmatic and/or bigoted viewpoints may well prove to be a public health hazard far greater that AIDS itself'.[31]

Dr John Habgood, the Anglican Archbishop of York has made a notable and well-known comment which was widely repeated in 1988 from his Diocesan newspaper: 'The world faces a medical crisis. But it is also a moral crisis. It is not simply a crisis of sexual morality though restrained sexual behaviour is going to be increasingly important for the foreseeable future. The heart of the moral crisis is whether compassion and sensitivity and restraint towards one another can overcome fear, can encourage lifestyles which limit the spread of the disease, and can enable those inflicted with it to retain their dignity, and to die knowing they are upheld in faith and hope and love.'

Behind this outflow of Christian reflection on the AIDs crisis, there must surely be the theology of Christ's revolutionary attitude to the leper. Both the religious and governing establishment of the Jewish people saw the leper as cursed by God and to be kept out of the towns and villages by fear and ritual. This was not only a health regulation for social living but more importantly a moral obligation and imperative. Jesus cut his way through both theology and fear to embrace and heal the leper. He encouraged conformity with the health regulations as established: the referral to the priests for judgment of freedom from the curse. His emphasis was on healing the body and so the first response of the Church to AIDS should be the Sacrament of the Sick.

The post-Vatican 11 restoration of caring for the body with the sacramental healing of Christ has still to be set free emphatically from the cleansing of the senses from that sin to which each of our senses can lead us, the Greek error that the body is evil or fundamentally imperfect and that a sacrament of God become man cannot centre on the corrupt human side of men and women. When this takes place, the sacrament will drive forward the Christian counselling approach which will open the way for the sacramental meeting with Christ and ensure that the despairing victim of AIDS will be enabled to listen to and hear Christ's word of healing and hope and find it reflected and embodied in the caring community of listeners and friends. The changes in the Sacrament of the Sick after Vatican 11 have still to be applied to every aspect of human sickness.

An Ad Clerum of the Bishops of London Dioceses in April 1987 is clear: 'If we belong to Christ and are entrusted with a share in His ministry, this includes touching those whom society treats as untouchable, and embracing those whom society isolates.'[32] Paul Clarke adds 'There is a real danger of a leper colony mentality, of an 'us-them' attitude developing when and if the disease reaches noticeable proportions.' And lastly Jim Cotter in *What Price Healing in a Time of Epidemic*:

> If they sense that we know deeply the trials of suffering and of dying, they will beat a path to our door, and we both may find a deeper healing in a wondrously strange exchange. We shall have become 'priests' in the only sense of the word that matters, living at the centre of sacrifice, the utter giving upon which the world depends for everything.[33]

This combines with the priesthood of all believers and with the sacramental role of the ministerial priest as we bring ourselves as Jesus did to say 'Behold I come to do your will'—'Not my will but thine be done'. For the AIDS victim and the care-ers this has a special significance for 'death as the last of the enemies of mankind to be overcome' has never been clearer.

I have met AIDS victims who have become so bitter that they have engaged on a campaign to infect as many others as they can, or who as prostitutes feel their clients have only themselves to blame. That bitterness I have found to be a very hollow bravado and a hatred of others only born out of despair and desperation. It is vulnerable to caring listening.

I have also met AIDs victims who have become saints because a priest and caring group in Edinburgh accepted them, spent time listening to them and enabled them to develop into the sort of uniquely caring human beings who perhaps only emerge out of the overcoming of fear, pain and hopelessness.

Such people made me ashamed that the Vatican conference on AIDS in November 1989 could be described as 'three days of gay bashing' by some of the most involved participants. It was sad that fifty participants had to walk out and set up their own conference and that a priest victim of AIDS should be ejected— and that the scientist who discovered the AIDS virus ended cynically by declaring 'some of us don't believe in heaven'. One speaker was even allowed to describe AIDS as God's punishment of mankind for modern morality.'

On the other hand, the people I've known to struggle so bravely with AIDS give the lie to the sort of prejudice that led the inhabitants to turn the little village of Torphichen in Scotland into a fortress against a proposed AIDS hospice on the outskirts and marked its boundaries with ugly posters; and in the United States brought bitter resistance from the townspeople of the neighbouring counties to Elisabeth Kübler-Ross' plans to care on her farm for the AIDS virus infected babies nobody else wanted.

I'll leave the last word to Dr Kübler-Ross and her very special vision of AIDS victims which patient faithful listening can alone discern:

> With such enormous prejudice against AIDS patients, and
> fear of them, people lose sight of the fact that most—if not
> all—die an early death at a time when their lives have just

begun, when they are just starting to make their contribution to society. The gay movement has tried to enlighten us about the enormous contributions of homosexuals to our society but as far as AIDs is concerned, most of us are still in the Dark Ages.

We have been taught over endless time that love is stronger than anything else and can literally conquer all evil. If we are to believe all this, wouldn't it be simple to spend our joint energies and reserves (on every level) to organise a worldwide team, not only for research but for care centres, support groups, treatment centres, counselling centres and bereavement groups? It would create myriad jobs, a golden opportunity for lonesome old people, an educational chance for minorities, and a sense of 'working on a common goal towards a world family where men help for the betterment of mankind'[34]

An impossible dream? Only if we don't listen.

Homosexuality

Christian care-ers need to be sensitive to the fact that a sense of stigma can prevent homosexual men or women from hearing the words of those who wish to help them. The work of Quest and similar organisations for Catholic homosexuals, exists to counter the desperate feeling of being 'outside the pale' which is that of the Catholic homosexual. Parallels exist in other Christian Churches. The Church's teaching that sexual acts are only for within the marriage relationship cuts off the prospect of morally acceptable sexual activity to those who are convinced—rightly or wrongly—that by genes (and there is now some evidence) or by psychological development they can be nothing other than homosexual in their sexual orientation.

Some theologians have argued that sexual contacts in a stable homosexual relationship between consenting adults can be squared in exceptional circumstances with Christian morality in terms of being 'the lesser of two evils' or 'the best an individual can manage within the limitations of their situation'. This is not acceptable to mainstream Roman Catholic morality or to traditional Protestant values, but even within the most rigid Christian positions there are nuances.

44

Homosexual feelings are generally regarded as common for most individuals at some stage of their development and, when they are condemned as 'unnatural and disgusting', the paradox is that the likelihood of these feelings becoming established and developing into exclusively homosexual affective life is increased and not diminished. To encourage people to let these thoughts come and go—like a video playing in the background—is not to betray Christian morality but to understand the pattern of muddled human thought patterns. Again too, it has to be quite deliberately argued out, against people's prejudices, that a person with homosexual orientation is just as capable of non-sexual but close relationships with friends of the same sex and of celibate living as is the heterosexual in terms of celibacy and friendships with the opposite sex. The spiritual advice about the dangers involved in 'particular friendships' put more sexual ideas into people's heads than it ever prevented!

When realism makes the Christian care-er face the frequency of sexual contacts among the homosexual community as it does in the heterosexual community, the same question arises of how serious these offences against mainstream moral positions are in the individual who is trying to live in a situation of stigma and increasing isolation. Again too, when homosexual men or women are finding it impossible to live up to the Christian standards they themselves accept, it is important not to block for them a way back to the community and community values by so reinforcing their guilt as to turn it into despair. In this as in so many other areas the Christian community has to find ways to continue caring for people where they are, acknowledging the mystery of what any individual can rise to in terms of morality at any particular time. Non-judgmental Christian caring and a caring which does not impose pre-conditions must surely be a better vision of Christ than a rigid attitude that we'll do this if you conform in this way or that . . . but otherwise 'Well we're sorry'.

Divorce

Catholic Marriage Advisory Centres have transformed the position for many married couples facing up to the contrasts between the ideals which brought them together in marriage, the ideals reinforced in Christian teaching that love, prayer and God's grace can solve every situation, and the reality (in Britain) that one in three will divorce and another one in three will only stay together for the sake of the children or convenience. CMAC non-directive counselling has enabled countless couples to grow in their love , to heal what has gone wrong and thus allow the 'domestic Church' to be a centre of God's transforming power set free from human obstacles.

It is nothing short of tragic that priests can still tell married couples to go away and pray about it—without even spending the time to listen to allow some of the hidden things to unravel. The sense of failure and guilt is a real crucifixion for those for whom things don't work out. All too often people stay in situations of desperately destructive pain because they took him or her for better, for worse. . . . A deeper listening to divorced or divorcing people by the celibate witnesses who still predominantly shape theology would force us to look again with greater pastoral urgency at the whole canonical morass of annulment and the impossibility of presenting a pastoral solution to divorced people (being able to go to communion in the 'private forum' by going to another church where the danger of scandal will be avoided) as anything other than a reinforcement of the feeling of stigma rather than the sense of release it is intended to achieve. Surely a way can be found to renew our witness to the Christian ideal of total unconditional commitment to married love while at the same time allowing Christ's forgiveness of the sinner 'not seven times but seventy times seven' to become a felt reality in pastoral care.

The Association of Divorced and Separated Catholics in the UK, and its parallel groupings in other Churches and in other countries, centres on a feeling of stigma and failure which can be just as complete and traumatic for those who are divorced as that experienced by homosexuals. And yet those who have not experienced that feeling of being an outcast would maintain with great honesty and conviction that this is a nonsense and they have nothing but sympathy for the victims of divorce. When one third of married people in a congregation are divorced, sermons on Christian marriage have to be radically revised to stop reinforcing that stigma in the most vulnerable of the married people being addressed; pastoral visiting has to be incredibly sensitive; and the contact between the pastor and the separated, divorced or remarried has to become dramatically more thoughtful.

An analysis of the annulment procedures for those Catholics who are divorced and either want to remarry or have already remarried 'outside the Church' will again point to the need for pastors and care-ers to be aware that most people in such a situation hesitate to ask for their case to be put to the Marriage Tribunal even if they are aware of this as a possibility. The reason is normally either humility or an enfeebling sense of failure. It is only long slow patient listening which will allow possible reasons for annulment to emerge: they won't be presented as facts. Even when there is no hope of proving grounds for an annulment, the ground for the establishment of a 'pastoral solution', a 'good-conscience marriage' to allow a remarried couple to go to the sacraments, can only be established by long patient sensitive listening and will be blocked out before it starts by an opening which 'lays out the hard facts'. Too many people live with those hard facts for the rest of their lives, because the lack of a counselling approach in the priest asked to give the facts has established an insurmountable intellectual and emotional barrier in the couple to finding a place again in Christ's Church community. Dom Edmund Flood has written beautifully of the issue for the British situation.[35] A useful question and answer outline can be found in *Catholics and Broken Marriage* by John T. Catoir[36]

Mental Handicap and Mental Illness

For those who work with either the mentally handicapped or the mentally ill, it is a constant source of amazement how often attitudes to these two groups become hopelessly confused. The mentally ill are treated as mentally retarded and the slow learners are treated as mentally ill. These two attitudes are equally damaging.

The confusion goes back a long way. In fact it can be traced to a much worse state of confusion which formed the thought patterns in which Jesus' ministry took place. Both the mentally ill and the mentally handicapped were to one degree or another treated as having been cursed by God or having been possessed by the devil. Our Lord responded to that not by producing a set of psychological insights from the twentieth century—which would have violated the reality of his Incarnation in that particular time and place—but by bringing his accepting and healing work to 'casting out the devils' in exactly the same way

47

as He healed physical illness. What we have to do is realise that 'being possessed by the devil' is primitive fear describing what lies outside human understanding and experience—but it's only the language categories which are wrong. The reality of Jesus healing all human illness is what's important.

In our day, we have to make clear that the mentally handicapped are not mentally ill and furthermore that mental handicap is not in itself a physical illness—even though it may be accompanied by a physical illness. The people once labelled as mentally handicapped are better described as people with learning difficulties: for a wide variety of reasons, they are slower to learn than the average. What they need is listening ... and time. Lots of time. To give them the Sacrament of the Sick and to arrange Mass services for them in which they are jollied along can be misguided, desperately patronising and deeply wounding. To describe them as innocents or refuse to confront them with the things they do wrong is to insult them and hinder their moral development. Listening must be a learning process for both the slow to learn and the care-er. Jean Vanier's books should be required reading, especially when he faces the most difficult problems such as those of human sexuality. His way is not everyone's problems such as those of human sexuality. His way is not everyone's and his solutions are by no means universally agreed but his attitude of Christian caring has much to teach us all.[37]

When we think of the mentally ill, one of the most frightening contrasts is at visiting hour at the Mental Hospital when compared with visiting hour at the General Hospital. The General Hospital is crowded, the Mental Hospital is not. People are afraid to admit to mental illness but boast of their operation scars. The person who suffers mental illness is also cursed with the nasty feeling that it is somehow his or her fault, that a little more effort would have averted the breakdown. Much has to do with Health Education and poor investment in Mental Health but the Church has to face major questions. Those of us who fought to have the Sacrament of the Sick used for mental illness, and then rejoiced to see the use built into the new rite, are still disappointed by the lack of automatic connection of the sacrament with mental illness when it is so well established for physical illness. In this area too, improved sacramental theology and liturgical practice could give the lead to the development of a pastoral practice which would have much more listening to the mentally ill and far less rushing in with words of 'sweet advice' that in the painful associations of mental illness can be almost entirely counter-productive to a communication of Christian caring and Good News.

Concluding Reflections

This long chapter has only touched on some of the major areas of human crisis which the Churches seem to deal with very badly. An increasingly middle class membership likes to pretend that a mere belonging to the Church or a handing out of black and white principles solves all the problems. Old theology and old attitudes make Christ's command that we need fresh wineskins for fresh wine all the more urgent. In each and every one of these areas of crisis, it seems to me that we pastors do not listen enough—and so miss the chance to communicate Christ's forgiving, healing and transforming love to a modern generation that thirsts for these realities but often feels excluded from them. The fundamental question for Christian care-ers is how Jesus would react to the sort of challenges arising from all these modern human situations.

2

Christian Care-ers and the Mass Media

A Radio or Television Counselling Ministry

THE WORLD of today has been characterised as a 'global village' because of the impact of radio and television. If Christ related to people individually and sensitively in the villages of Palestine with an approach which can only be likened today to that of the counsellor, the challenge in the global village for those who wish to continue Christ's work is the challenge of Christian counselling in the media. It is a wide question of approach for all those who engage in the dialogue of minds and hearts that is mass media communication, but here we will confine ourselves to exploring the ways in which the ones who wish to be Christian care-ers in the mass media should respond to the needy and troubled.

The document on the Mass Media which emerged as a follow-up to the Vatican II Decree on the Instruments of Social Communication (Inter Mirifica) is illuminating. It describes Christ as the perfect communicator under six heads:

1) He identified himself with his audience.
2) He gave his message with the whole manner of his life.
3) He spoke from within and spoke out of the press of his people.
4) He spoke without fear or compromise.
5) He adjusted to the way of speaking of and to the thought patterns of his audience.
6) He spoke out of the predicament of their time.[1]

This chapter will argue that this picture of Christ can be incarnated in a very special way in the Christian counsellor on television or particularly radio (since it is the medium of the lonely). It will also argue that this very unusual embodiment of Christian caring has many lessons for the way we all try to be other Christs for those around us.

50

One major preliminary obstacle emerges. This is the fact that if one is to be in the global village what Christ was in the Palestinian village, it is necessary to do so by being what is pejoratively described as a celebrity. Despite the fact that Christ communicated interactively by being a personality who was talked about, the accepted prejudice and presumption in most areas of Christianity is that the Christian should avoid being such a personality—in the cause of 'humility'. This ignores the constant humiliation and burden of being a personality (which seems to echo St Paul's humiliation!) and the fact that Mark's device of the 'Messianic secret' was never in practice a pastoral rule for Jesus, but at most a prudent effort not to be misunderstood as a guerilla leader against the Roman occupation and was in the end a dramatic failure, which made his message effective though bringing about his final hour of death and resurrection.

In modern broadcasting terms, Dr Willie Barclay in the sixties and seventies was resented in Church circles for being a personality. At the BBC before and during the second World War, Dr James Welsh subsumed this question into his fight against a 'BBC religion' and a 'Church of the air.' Thus, despite the intervention of the Prime Minister Neville Chamberlain, he got rid of Canon Elliot for becoming a celebrity. John Phelan put the general principle very well in *Mediaworld* in 1977:

> If a celebrity is a celebrity because he is celebrated, an opinion is persuasive, an idea is important, an ideal is worthy because it is endorsed by a celebrity. In a way, the celebrity invests the things related to him with, not surprisingly, celebrity. To produce a movie, get a star. To sell soap, get a star. To save a soul, get a star. To be heard, get a star.[2]

For the Christian, Christ is the real star. The Christian broadcaster must say with John the Baptist 'He must increase, I must decrease'; and the person who is considering being a Christian counsellor on radio or television will be only too glad to leave Christ to take over the immense mountain ranges of human need he or she will encounter. In more general terms, however, Colin McArthur in *Television and History* underlines the way in which abstract material can be transformed by a warm personality:

> The locating of a narrator in the actual substance of his narration offers a quasi-talismatic guarantee of truth: the place

51

actually exists, therefore what is said in that place is true. This was nothing to do with history and everything to do with television. What we are seeing is television—and specifically the well financed co-production series—displaying its resources.[3]

Dr Ronald Falconer spoke warmly in this connection of Dr Selby Wright, the famous radio padre: 'He was friendly and pleasant to listen to; the listener felt he was speaking directly and personally to him; he spoke about everyday problems which worried not only servicemen and women, but even more, their fathers, mothers, wives and sweethearts.' Audiences, he said, had severe standards for religious communicators (how much more for religious counsellors on the media?): they must be human but 'It must be attractive humanity, slightly larger than life, perhaps, but nevertheless with complete integrity: for the meretricious takes in no-one.' He expects his communicator to be a man of God, not parading it but revealing it in what he says and in his attitudes.[4]

One of the problems in all religious broadcasting is that religiously based personalities seem mostly to have been suckered by the religious label. They adopt the 'holy voice' and thus look and sound uncomfortable. They either try too hard or are so laid back as to disappear. Forced jollity makes them the ideal target for the satirist—good fun but too near the truth to be comfortable. If the Church is to respond to the demands of the global village, it will have to produce genuine religiously based personalities who stand outside the middle class gob-stopped caricature. And if the search succeeds? Andrew M. Greeley in his otherwise undistinguished novel *Lord of the Dance* highlights what would no doubt happen, when he portrays Fr John Farrell— a television chat-show star—discovering his name is missing from an archdiocesan workshop on communication and being forced to complain: 'The Church and the archdiocese have been my life since I first went to the seminary almost thirty years ago. Everything I've done has been directed to the service of the archdiocese, I didn't want to take the talk show. And now they all think I'm on an ego trip and have begun to pretend I don't exist . . . I simply don't understand it.'[5]

To be a religious counsellor on television would undoubtedly bring such tensions. On radio there is more anonymity and it is this less celebrity-based experience which will be used in this chapter to illustrate the general theme of being a counselling career as a Christian. It is based on ten years' experience working as 'Andy' on a local radio late night counselling programme called *Open Line*. *Open Line* is quite different from similar programmes which have mushroomed in America with psychologists such as Dr Toni Grant of KABC Los Angeles, or the psychiatrist Dr Philip Hodson on LBC in London. It is a million light years away from the brisk combative chat of Anna Raeburn on Capital Radio in London. It is philosophically and theologically the very opposite of the evangelically counselling programmes (which are back-up practical help for those who have been 'converted' and into which vast sums of money are being poured in America's religious channels). Again too it is deliberately less overtly religious than the programme run by the priest who is perhaps most famous for his work in religious radio counselling, Fr Jim McLaren from Australia. His description of his role is helpful:

> The presence of a priest on radio, talking to people about their everyday lives, is very similar to the confessional. It ranges from the banal to the spiritual, from the passing frustrations to the deeply rooted torments and from the simple moral questions to the profound conscience. They are looking for acceptance and healing and react strongly when I sound judgmental. The expectation is to have me guide and comfort them but never condemn. Some of the old guard Church people expect a moral judgment on every caller—'why didn't you tell it was a sin?' is the kind of comment. My own feeling about the 'sin' must not prevent a caller from finding an answer. He does not need a theological judgment but real Christian support. In many cases the person is not looking for a Church reaction but a human response which is concerned and caring. He is not meeting a congregation but the community at large.

When Pierre Babin analysed with him the power for good of the programme, two important conclusions were agreed on: the power of the human voice ('My sheep hear the sound of my voice') and the building of community. Pierre described the community of care, practical help, prayer and advice as a kind of 'Church' likened to the gathering outside church on Sunday mornings to discuss common concerns.[6]

The *Open Line* has myself as a priest as one of the anonymous counsellors who speak in the quiet of the night to anonymous callers as one human being to another. It has then more restrictions as to the Christian word which can be uttered, but this discipline—based as it is on respect for the opinions of others—does not seem at the end of the day to limit the witness to Christ's healing but rather to facilitate its acceptability. It may have more lessons for voicing Christ's words to a world which has walked away from inadequate versions of his way of life than much more explicit preaching of 'the message'. At the end of the day it would seem to be the discipline of counselling which best describes the Christian rationale of the approach.

The Open Line—an Experiment which has worked

Aims and Beginnings

The *Open Line* programme has been broadcast from Edinburgh by Radio Forth since 1978 and is now broadcast on MAX-AM, Radio Tay and Radio Borders. It began after a traumatic local community experience and a dramatically successful Radio Forth response to the crisis. The whole of 'Forth country' was cut off by snow over New Year at a time when the road gritters and snow-ploughs were in the midst of an industrial dispute. Radio Forth responded with a 'Snowline' manned by the voluntary presence of pretty well the whole station staff. It proved that people saw the station as a 'friend on the air'. Those in need phoned in with their problems and those able to help phoned in to offer immediate practical assistance. After it was all over, the company decided to establish a programme which would continue the same spirit. They turned to the Religious Programmes Department with its balance of station professionalism and the committed volunteers from the Edinburgh and District Churches' Council for Local Broadcasting to produce it. This Christian commitment which was present at the origins of the programme has ensured the motivation and caring that—from the Christian base or another—is essential to undertaking the responsibility of such a programme.

The aim of the programme has been to provide a 'friend on the air' for lonely and troubled people at a time in the weekend when people feel particularly alone with their problems. What has resulted was summed up by a letter from one thirty-five year old spinster towards the end of the first year: 'One genuine friendly person really interested in another's problems can put an entirely different outlook onto a person's life.' More quantifiable results are seen by the fact that one referral of a troubled person to a group can result in half a dozen turning up that week for help or support. Other letters flood in saying that they had never phoned but that they were sitting trapped with their problem and happened to hear us talking to someone with the same circumstances. Several said that they had been sitting with a bottle of tablets ready to swallow the lot when they were given a new way of looking at life through listening to the programme.

The audience multiplied the listening figures from the programme previously in that slot by eight to fourteen times over the three hours and increased by a thousand per cent when the programme was extended to a neighbouring radio station. This has been true even though it has eschewed any attempt at audience building and in fact often perseveres with calls when the audience switch-off point may well have been long gone in normal radio terms.

It is important to make clear that in no sense did the programme set out to provide a social work agency on the air or professional counselling. Instead it aims to be the radio equivalent of the good friend you'd never realised lived next door, or the stranger who's confided in because he or she seems a sympathetic listener. The genuine seeker of help calls the station because he or she already knows it as a friend and as a source of unbiased personal and private advice. The caller, however, is under no pressure to act on the advice and at every stage in the conversation remains totally in control. Unlike other professional givers of help to whom the person might turn, there is no demand that the person goes into a weakness, dependency situation. The caller calls the tune and at every point has the ultimate sanction of hanging up the phone. The programme is and is perceived to be part and only part of the helping service provided by the station throughout day-time programming. It goes out of its way to stress that the counsellors don't have all the answers to their own problems and far less to anyone else's problems. It clearly points away from itself to the resources the caller has available but cannot see as being helpful at that moment—this begins with their families and opens out to all the caring agencies in the area. In other words, it is a bridge of connection between people: between the people who need help and the people who can give help.

All these qualifications and limitations are crucial if the programme is to be a success. To try to do too many things would be disastrous and would be an impertinent attempt to duplicate badly what is done well already in the community. The *Open Line* programme has been acutely aware at all times of what Robert McLeish in his excellent training book for local radio observes: 'Of all the programmes which a station puts on, this is the one where real damage may be done if the broadcaster gets it wrong. Discussing problems of loneliness, marriage and sex or the despair of a would-be suicide has to be taken seriously.'[7]

The fundamental objection to programmes of this kind is that they exploit individual problems, or rather individuals who have problems, and exploit them for the gross purpose of public entertainment. In this, the critics would say, it panders to the aural equivalent of the voyeur—though surely the voyeurism envisaged would be of the most harmless type imaginable. Again too it would be all too easy to condemn the programme for providing a forum for the exhibitionist streak in human nature, even though it is an anonymous exhibitionism. This—to quote Robert McLeish again—'depends on how the programme is handled, the level of advice offered and whether there is a genuine attempt at caring'.[8] Clearly this is a difficult area to self-assess, but the responses of listeners and professionals alike have been immensely supportive and so a confidence in the value of what is being done has grown up over the years. A description of what happens will not give the reader all the answers, for so much of what happens takes place 'between the lines' and is ultimately inexpressible.

The *Open Line* is on the air between eleven o'clock on a Saturday night and two o'clock on a Sunday morning. This is the time of night and the night of the week when people can be at their most lonely. It is a combination of knowing that so many are out enjoying themselves and realising that the next day the routine of life is suspended, the shops and streets are relatively empty and the emptiness of the weekend stretches out interminably. It is essentially a phone-in programme and so has to face the objection that fifty per cent of British homes have no phone. In point of fact, the number who phone from phone boxes is extremely heartening: because of the 'pips' and because they are likely to be poorer callers and because there is no intrusion to their privacy as such by phoning back, these callers are phoned back before they go on air.

For those who prefer not to phone, or find it difficult, there is also a time for answering letters on air. This has been expanded recently into a daily letters spot in the morning and very success-fully opens out the care-ing to a different audience. In general the letters format proves helpful in a quite different but very real way. It does not have the immediate contact and so is an even greater searching out into the dark, but it gives the opportunity of a more studied listening to every nuance in the written com-munication. For the person writing it is even more anonymous than making a call and obviously less frightening. Writing things down is always encouraged on the programme anyway, and it is clear that in one sense the letters are skills learned from having listened to the programme and in another sense they are part of a much wider dialogue which goes on between the presenters talking on the *Open Line* and the person listening. Thus the letters continue the one-to-one sharing of the telephone calls. With the letters as with the phone calls, we make clear the limitations of the programme. We do not enter into correspon-dence because this would be a different role—and could in any case escalate to a position where the counsellor's health would be threatened or where additional personnel would have to be recruited and then trained. Exceptions are made but not advertised!

Anonymity is also seen as crucial. The two presenters are introduced and known by their first names only. Callers have to give their names and numbers to the back-up team for legal reasons but use their first name or a pseudonym on air. This first-name-only rule is to protect them and others. In general, ano-nymity is vital in all that happens: identifying elements are set aside as much as it possible to do so and emphasis is placed regularly on how easy it is for listeners to guess wrongly at the identity of callers. Accents on a phone line are blurred and circumstances in family situations are remarkably similar. This attempt at protection is helped by people genuinely recounting how they have been approached as having been on the programme when in fact they had at that stage never even heard of the programme.

For legal and technical reasons, the whole programme goes out on delay: in other words, what is spoken is held back and broadcast some few seconds afterwards so that, by jumping from 'delayed time' back into 'real time', the presenter can cut out libellous, obscene or damaging utterances before they are heard on air. 'Sorry we seem to have lost that call' is the usual under-statement, but occasionally it is used as an opportunity to ask the hoax caller to reflect on why they phoned and what it tells them about themselves that they abused our trust on a pro-gramme which serves so many needy people. Abuse and hoax are remarkably infrequent. They are politely set aside or used as an opportunity to talk to the many listeners who will be suffering genuinely from the pain that was the subject chosen to be raised by the hoaxer.

Staffing Challenges and Programme Development
The history of those who have staffed the *Open Line* over its first ten years is revealing. One of Radio Forth's popular pre-senters, Hazel Fowlie, had a caring image for the listeners so when the programme was launched she was given the task of hosting the three hour Saturday night phone in (23.00–2.00). Behind the scenes, there was an engineer in charge of con-trolling the sound production, one helper answering the phones and another relaying messages to the studio to give the presenter some written information of what was coming on the phone lines. On air, Hazel was to be accompanied by two counsellors. As the priest responsible for the successful religious programme *View from Earth* (also presented by Hazel Fowlie, a tie-up which is an important link in maximising the contribution of the motivation of the religious programming staff) I was asked to be a regular counsellor, working closely with Hazel to oversee the presentation. Ron was asked to be the other counsellor because of his commitment as a Church of Scotland elder and a selfless social work organiser for the Churches. His busy schedule necessitated regular substitutes and this developed until there were four people doing a rota, with myself as the resident counsellor. Three of these were experienced as counsellors in other fields and were women. Soon it became clear that the

balance of what was offered was better with one male and one female counsellor.

The next phase of development came when Hazel and her husband—who did the vital monitoring first answer to the call behind the scenes—had to leave the *Open Line* for personal reasons. The religious programming staff, particularly Joan from *View from Earth* and later Anne, filled the behind-the-scenes vacuum; to preserve the vital continuity I, as the resident counsellor over the years, was asked to present the programme while continuing to work on it as a counsellor. This was taken up with the managing director over the head of the programme controller by three of the rota of counsellors; the other, a consultant psychiatrist was not involved and disassociated herself from what happened when she learned about it later.

The substance of the complaint made by the three counsellors illustrated a question which faces all such counselling programmes on either radio or television and so must be dealt with. They were trying to take the principles of the neutrality of the counsellor in the counselling process into the new situation of the quite different counselling on radio or television, where the callers contact a person whom they have had the opportunity to get to know very well in the anonymity of the contact between broadcaster and listener or viewer. It is unique, however, in that they phone the person they know—not a counselling service. For better or for worse (and it will be one or other in every different situation) the 'who' of the radio or television counsellor is vital. Added to that, the link established between presenter and audience will shape what happens with the counsellors. They are dependent on how the whole programme comes across and this depends on the link forged by the one who carries the main burden of presentation. In this there are parallels with the caring of the whole Christian parish and the vital realisation that all the caring involvement of lay people in a parish can be badly handicapped if the 'presenter' is not communicating the right caring message! Far more often than is realised, the personality of the 'presenter' is of more importance than any of us pastors would like to believe. God became man . . . and still lives among us in that way.

Be that as it may, the issue argued by the counsellors to the managing director was that the fact that I was presenting and counselling on the programme would undermine the professional counselling taking place by giving me too high a profile. In view of their distinguished work in the field of counselling, the managing director brought in a substitute presenter for some months. This, however, was adjudged a failure in the sense of preserving the uniqueness of the programme. It was decided that I should present the programme as originally planned.

At this stage, the three counsellors from the rota to accompany me chose to leave rather than continue. Because the reasons on which the decision was made were 'radio' reasons rather than 'counselling' reasons, they then wrote to all the referral agencies in the area appealing for support in a campaign which claimed that Radio Forth had decided to lower counselling standards for the sake of good radio. This of course is a fundamental misunderstanding of what good radio is. It is a one-to-one mutually respectful contact or it is nothing. The problem underpinning this misunderstanding is the attempt to apply normal counselling practice—which rightly underplays the personality of the counsellor, though arguably unrealistically!—to the quite different radio situation where people only choose to listen or phone in because of the trust bond already established with the personality/personalities at the heart of the programme.

At this point, we were fortunate to acquire the services of Helen as resident counsellor, with other women counsellors substituting for her. She herself was a minister of the United Free Church and a trained social worker. She proved to be invaluable to the programme and must take a great deal of the credit for what developed. Following the change in format, the audience was retained, the feedback from monitoring listening groups was favourable to the change, calls at the switchboard increased dramatically and then steadily, and listening comment was pretty uniformly complimentary.

The back-up personnel remained at first along the original lines. An engineer was in overall charge of the technical quality. With an average of thirty-one calls to be dealt with, commercials and music to be fitted in at appropriate (and unobjectionable) points and a flow of conversation to be maintained, it was felt that the presenter had enough to do without having to worry about the technical control. Nowadays, I do the technical control also since I am well used to the situation. This has proved to be an advantage, though at first it was frightening. There is an immediacy about direct control of the balance of sound: the person at the end of the line with the studio sound, and then with the music. To bring up the fader is an outward sign of the effort that is needed in *Open Line* to reach out to the other person and establish real contact. Paradoxically that is what makes the passive listening possible. It is for me a modern parable and illustration of what many of us as priests or pastors or care-ers fail to do effectively in normal pastoral contact. A good listener must make the active effort to bring in the other person: he or she must learn every technique in the book to eliminate the things about himself or herself which put other people off (and that needs self-reflection and prayer . . . and good friends to be honest with us) and then work hard to make it easy for the other person to come in.

Behind the scenes we still have two others answering the phones, weeding out imposters, helping callers to clarify what they wish to talk about—at least in general terms. The principal here is Joan, an elder of the Church of Scotland. The demands of patience, tolerance, firmness and caring are just as heavy on those working behind the scenes. They underline the importance of everyone in a parish or pastoral community in enabling others to talk to the priest or minister by allowing them to find the words with which they will feel more confident in their initial approach.

In addition, there is a small group of carefully vetted volunteers who would be prepared to do counselling off-air for those still in need of counselling help. This would have been built up as needs demanded but it is significant how callers seem satisfied, at least for the moment, with what takes place on air. Partly, this is a matter of their instinctive acceptance of the limitations of the medium, but it is particular to the *Open Line* broadcasting in its own local situation where there is a wide range of caring services in both the public and voluntary sector. It would be wrong and pretentious for a radio station to duplicate these. In other situations, however, it might well be the duty of Christian volunteers committing themselves to an *Open Line* type of programme to commit themselves also, as members of the Churches, to provide the back-up services without which a programme such as this would be a cruel deceit.

In due course, Helen moved to another part of Scotland but her work had so strengthened the pattern that again we were fortunate to secure the help of Sheila as resident counsellor, with Judy and Rosemary presently substituting as circumstances demand. The balance of man and woman counsellor on the programme I would now see as integral to what we do. Hazel for the beginning, Helen for the rebirth, Sheila for continuing that new life, and the consultant woman psychiatrist who has given unstinting support in the background, all share what there is of achievement in what happens on *Open Line*. Others too in the background are unsung facilitators of its continuance.

The spread of problems has been quite remarkable. Fears that we would get bogged down in sex or drink have proved unfounded and we have been far freer from 'regular' callers than any other normal station programme. Thus we have another clear indication of the acceptance by listeners of the limitations of the programme and a welcome absence of the dependency factor of other types of counselling.

Almost by definition, 'early line' phone calls for the purpose of shaping the programme are not appropriate, though of course in other types of phone in programmes they are ideal: this will become clear as we analyse exactly what sort of counselling contact is involved on *Open Line*. Concentration on making a programme in this way would limit our objective of having the focus firmly fixed on the present loneliness and worry of the listeners. The programme emerges from their immediate situation. It is the old pastoral adage that people mostly have to be attended to when they ask rather than when we can arrange a 'convenient' appointment.

In the earlier days, gaps between calls used to be filled with conversation about the general worries that were mirrored in the news media during the previous week. This was a useful tool in finding echoes in listeners. They were reassured to find people talking about the things they were talking about at work or in the pub—or, more significantly, what they heard others talking about in the pub while they felt excluded. This element, how-ever, has largely disappeared because of the pressure of calls. It is a loss but the immediacy of the calls more than compensates. The three hours generally fly past with far more callers jamming the lines than we could possibly talk to. In one sense this is desperately regrettable, but it has the good side effect of easing out many of the less urgent or even frivolous calls. It's the old situation that what you lose on the swings you gain on the roundabouts! Again too we used to use thoughtfully worded songs to fill the gaps. The only song that remains is one to close the programme and even it is squeezed week after week by the pressure of what is more urgent. That is as it should be.

Crises or community felt emotions are the only exception to the total concentration on callers and letters. It would be wrong to broadcast a programme that builds bridges of caring and then ignore events such as the Piper Alpha tragedy, the Hillsborough and Lockerbie disasters or the slaughter of the Chinese students in Beijing. They are always talked about as the context within which we can share the problems which are immediately and critically ours, with decisions to be made moment by moment which will make those problems worse or better. People prove to be enormously sensitive to the problems of others even when trapped or frightened by their own. They are overwhelmed by them and often feel guilty about speaking of their own 'lesser problems' and have to be reassured about the rightness of their continuing to express their own pain against that background. All in all the interchange can be a really humbling and rewarding element of the *Open Line* programme.

Analysis of the Open Line

It is often more difficult to articulate the essence of what's happening in a situation of human interaction than it is to describe or to decide—having listened—that it is effective in providing a valuable service to the community. This is true of the *Open Line* but some attempt must be made to analyse it if only to expose the lessons inherent in its effectiveness.

Counselling
Counselling of some kind is clearly at the heart of the *Open Line*. It is not, however, professional counselling: and that by aim and object. What sort of counselling is it . . . and can it be justified?

Dietrich Bonhoeffer gives the Christian setting. 'Many people are looking for an ear that will listen. They do not find it among Christians because Christians are talking when they should be listening. He who no longer listens to his brother will soon be no longer listening to God either. . . One who cannot listen long and patiently will presently be talking beside the point and

63

never really speaking to the other, albeit he be not conscious of it.[9] Proverbs 23:19 is succint and to the point: A wise person learns by listening.

To counsel, in my view, is to befriend in order to help or advise someone, and to do so with deep respect for the mystery that is every human being and with a deep sense of privilege at what is shared. Who can do it? Jerome Frank, professor of psychiatry at Johns Hopkins University has written that 'anyone with a modicum of human warmth, common sense, some sensitivity of human problems and a desire to help can benefit many candidates for psychotherapy'.[10] Roger F. Hurding of Bristol suggests five qualities for such 'man-in-the-street-counselling'. They are:

experience of affliction
empathy
being a good listener
being non-judgmental
being persistently faithful.[11]

Such basic qualities are obviously needed in *Open Line* counselling, but much more is needed because it is now to be exercised publicly in a very specialist situation.

In my view, *Open Line* counselling is an amalgam of the normal skill of being a good listener with five more specialist forms of counselling:

crisis counselling
telephone counselling
anonymous counselling
radio counselling
breakthrough counselling

Each of these must be looked at quite carefully, first of all the art and skill of listening itself.

Listening

Listening is not something which comes naturally. Even the good listener of common parlance would have a good deal to learn from looking at some of the many principles involved in the most constructive types of listening. It's far from being a passive activity and one of the most helpful lists of the basic principles makes that clear. It came originally from a professor of communications at Fordham University:

1. Be interested and show it
2. Tune in to the other person
3. Hold your fire: don't jump at the first opportunity
4. Look for the main ideas in what's being poured out
5. Watch for the feelings which lie beneath what's been said
6. Monitor your own feelings and points of view
7. Notice non-verbal communication
8. Give the other person the benefit of the doubt
9. Work at listening
10. Get feedback

All of this makes it clear that listening is establishing a relationship with another person, a relationship of deep respect, a two-way relationship. In his book *Telephone Counselling* Gordon Hambly quotes Fr Clive Litten as to the extraordinary things which happen when I am listened to from the heart.

* I come alive * growth occurs * walls disintegrate
* I feel valued * I reveal my undiscovered uniqueness
* the healing process begins.[12]

The significance of the whole process of listening, in allowing people to come to see themselves more clearly and to value themselves more, is summed up by John Powell in *The Secret of Staying in Love*: 'No one can know what he looks like until he sees his reflection in some kind of mirror. It is an absolute human certainty that no one can know his own beauty or perceive a sense of his own worth until it has been reflected back to him in the mirror of another loving caring human being.'[13]

Crisis Counselling
Crisis counselling is an aspect of counselling which has its origins in the work of Dr Erich Lindeman in 1944 in Massachusetts General Hospital; also Anton Boisen writing in the twenties about the relationship of religious experience and mental disorder, and Gerald Caplan working with Lindeman from 1946 on. Erika Erickson and Lydia Rapoport have developed and systematised this work:

'There are three sets of inter-related factors that can produce a state of crisis:
a) a hazardous event which poses some threat;

65

b) a threat to instinctual need which is symbolically linked to earlier threats that resulted in vulnerability or conflict;

c) an inability to respond with coping mechanisms.'[14]

This description I have found to correspond with much of what I encounter on the *Open Line* and so I use it as a working definition. The consequence of the approach is that while the external situation doesn't necessarily form the crisis it must be respected as if if did because it has the initial associations. The approach of these authors then leaves aside the categories producing the stress, and goes on to see three questions as confirming the crisis situation when they are answered positively:

1. Has there been a recent onset of troublesome feelings and/or behaviour?
2. Have they tended to get progressively worse?
3. Can the onset be linked with some happening?

Yes to these questions means that he or she is at the stage of either:

going under   *or*   achieving rapid change or growth

This is paralleled by the Chinese ideogram for a crisis:

Danger   *or*   Opportunity

Time after time on the *Open Line*, the simple opening out with the caller of the fact that she or she is facing such a double-headed crisis—with inbuilt hope as well as threat—has helped the person to feel a sense of being understood . . . and of being able to progress further in understanding the pressure which has so frightened them in the quiet of the night.

Caplan concludes his study by declaring that people in crisis are more open to influence by others than they are at any other time. Their emotional equilibrium is upset, their thinking is unclear and so a relatively minor influence can give immense help or do great damage.[15] If the Saturday night hypothesis is correct (as a moment summing up the build-up of the past week, a time of loneliness and stress) and the person in distress hasn't been able to turn with fulfilment to anyone else, then the *Open Line* fits in as a crucial point in such crisis: and it has been my experience that it does. Its main value is in nudging the person back towards the coping mechanisms which will in turn affect the outcome of the crisis.

The goal of crisis counselling as described by the experts is threefold:

a) Symptom relief.
b) Actual growth through learning new coping methods.
c) The continuance of counselling.

All these are possible on the *Open Line*, except that the continuance of counselling element is the referral to another agency with a follow-up to the *Open Line* later being invited as an encouragement to the person to realise that objective.

A growing body of evidence (growing out of research begun by Rogers, continued by Truax and Carkhuff and elaborated by Carkhuff) suggests certain ingredients in successful counselling. These are described as 'facilitative conditions':

1. Accurate empathy and its accurate communication.
2. Respect.
3. Concreteness.
4. Genuineness.
5. Self-disclosure.
6. Confrontation without verbal shock treatment.
7. Immediacy in present relationships.[16]

Of these, the *Open Line* experience would confirm particularly vividly the danger and pointlessness of verbal shock treatment in relating with vulnerable people, the 'bruised reeds'—the one counsellor who tried this alienated the caller and irritated the listeners to the point of writing in to complain. The callers voted with their feet against such an approach. The centrality of a sense of immediacy in the present relationship of caller and counsellor has also been made crystal clear. People demand that they be helped *now* by *this* person. They are not unreasonable and do not expect to be given all the answers—far from it—but it is obvious that they call because they are able to do it then to this person—they could not have done it yesterday and they may well not be able to do it tomorrow. This has lessons for pastoral practice: the brusque response on the telephone or the 'blocking' housekeeper at the door often destroy the moment of grace for those in need.

67

For a Christian, of course, the high level of skill and awareness that should be developed in all counselling has to be secondary to the caring love that all counselling—whether inspired for secular or religious reasons—sees to be the essential ingredient. Gordon C. Hambly has a neat paraphrase of St Paul's chapter on love which is particularly thoughtful:

> If I verbalise all the best counselling principles but basically lack love or fail to demonstrate it, I am only sounding off. If I have insight into all kinds of wisdom and if I have power to effect change in the lives of others but have not love, I am nothing. If I spend everything I have to seek training and spend myself to the limit for others without love, I achieve nothing.

He goes on to suggest that 'to move gently and sensitively inside another person's world with unconditional caring and acceptance is to facilitate an atmosphere of loving trust to explore all that is there. The goal of this process as Jesus so powerfully expressed it is 'You will learn the truth and the truth shall make you free.' (Jn. 8:32)

When we consider that 'truth' in St John's writing would be better rendered as 'reality', as opposed to fiction and self-deception, this suggestion is perhaps even more accurate for what goes on in *Open Line* and what *Open Line* all too often reveals to be missing in ordinary pastoral practice within the Churches. It seems to link very directly with the traditional theology of the sacred Heart of Jesus, that compassionate love of Christ which invites us into a healing relationship with him in which he says 'Come to me all you who are over-burdened and I will give you rest'; and where 'imitation of Christ' means reflecting that accepting compassion as a challenge to the nature of everything we do as Christians.

The fact that so many people flood for help to the *Open Line* in their crisis—or write afterwards of how they had been helped by what was being said to someone else in a similar crisis—means that something is lacking in the service of the Church to those trapped in urgent crises of human need. It is at once chilling and humbling to read 'I was sitting with a glass of whisky and a bottle of pills determined to end it all when I put the radio on to keep me company . . . and I heard you talking quietly and patiently to someone who had just taken a massive overdose.

That was two years ago now but I still know that if I hadn't heard you in the middle of the night, I would not be here now and would not have got my life together again. It's been hard . . . but it's very special now.' For me, the people who represent Christ's visible presence must be so welcoming and available that the distressed will automatically turn to them by phone or in person when crisis threatens to overwhelm.

Telephone Counselling

Telephone counselling is now a well established and well researched phenomenon on the counselling scene. Lewis Rosenblum stresses that some people may be overwhelmed by the thought of personal contact but at the same time are seeking for some personal sustenance: 'The availability of voice contact is supremely important for them, for their own ventilation, for reassurance, to sustain the image that someone is there who cares.' He concludes: 'Telephone therapy deserves a legitimate place in the armamentarium of the therapist and the clinic. It should not be accorded second class status.'[19] Obviously, it can be used for preliminary counselling or follow-up counselling.

The *Open Line* lies firmly in the area of preliminary counselling and is run as such, but before moving on to a detailed outline of this it is probably important to draw the lesson inherent in telephone counselling for the work of the Christian pastor. Two questions arise. The first question is: how does the pastor answer the phone; are people welcomed into an immediate relationship or distanced or even rebuffed by the chill? All too often people go no further or, if they do, have stopped listening. The second question arises from this: if the pastor doesn't answer the phone, is the basic Christian outreach often vitiated by whoever does answer? Training of pastors and others in answering the phone is sadly neglected.

In *Breaking Point*, David K. Schwitzer sums up a great deal of the research which has been done.[20] The differences from normal counselling are crucial. The first is the absence of visual clues or stimuli with which to learn about the client so as to be able to help him or her. We cannot see the way the person cares for himself or herself physically, what the hands and eyes are doing and so on. The lack of all these clues demands much more sensitive and perceptive listening in order to be aware of the meaning of the tone of voice, its tremors and cracking, changes of pitch and volume, pace, sighs, choking etc. The other way round, the cues are also missing. Thus the weight falls on the counsellor's (and back-up personnel's) use of his or her voice. The quality makes a great difference: whether it is flat and monotone or alive and flexible, whining or shrill or well-rounded, too loud or too soft. Changes of the voice can convey warmth, caring and assurance *or* hardness, aloofness, off-handedness or brusque efficiency. Tone is not enough, however: explicit words must express to people, who by definition are not in the best of listening frames of mind, what would normally be conveyed in other ways by visual checking. Silences are also more likely to be threatening rather than therapeutic. It's worth remembering too that the client has a great deal of control: he or she can hang up at any time and there are far fewer social restraints to make it difficult to do so. The counsellor then has to abdicate the authority role and the controlling power.

All of this means that telephone counselling needs far more discipline than other forms. To quote Sue W. Brockop, 'The conversational model of transaction on the phone is worse than nothing at all with a person in crisis'. Thus the situation demands that the concentration be intense. This and other aspects of radio counselling proper means that in a three hour programme like the *Open Line*, two counsellors are better than one. To have more is confusing and destroys, to some extent at least, the one-to-one identification of good radio. To have less would probably mean that less would be given despite the fact that two means some loss of immediacy and one-to-one contact.

Anonymous Counselling

At first sight, this is a type of counselling which is not normal for pastoral work but it is more common than is generally realised. It is what takes place often on the phone if word goes round that this or that pastor is prepared to accept such calls. It takes place in the confessional, more dramatically in the traditional confessional box but at least partially in other situations. The *copia confessarium* law in the Roman Catholic Church which means that people should be provided with a confessor they don't know, at least once a year, is designed to give a degree of anonymity. In our increasingly mobile society, people take advantage of a degree of anonymity in approaching pastors. This should be sensitively respected and often is not.

The Telephone Samaritans, by the initiative of the Reverend Chad Varah, have come to provide an anonymous counselling service which has dramatically decreased the incidence of suicide. Its value is well documented elsewhere. An element of this clearly exists in the *Open Line* provision.

The radio audience is totally anonymous until they decide to phone in to the programme. At that point they risk losing their anonymity to some extent but the *Open Line* and similar programmes work hard at preserving the anonymity as far as possible.

As for the presenter, there is a mixture of notional anonymity and total exposure. At the beginning the identity of the counsellors was jealously preserved, partly to eliminate any element of reliance on their being 'authority figures'. This has broken down with myself due to the attacks on my presence on the programme, but continues with the other counsellor.

Personal identity is laid aside still for both of us, but who we are is our bridge to the listener. People phone to talk to someone they have tested out and accepted as a friend on the air. As already noted then, personality is central therefore to the service that is offered.

Radio Counselling

Though fairly new, the *Open Line* type of radio counselling has already achieved a certain number of basic principles. Perhaps the self-discipline these involve is the most powerful reminder they can give to the pastor. Watching out for the careless word—which can do such immense damage when uttered by a person with at least 'symbolic' authority to speak in the name of Christ—is a daily challenge to all of us in pastoral practice.

The first basic principle of radio counselling is that the role of the presenters is crucial. The demands are high. In Scotland, they must be familiar with the law of libel, the 'Rehabilitation of Prisoners' Act and the Scottish 'contempt of court' legislation which comes into play as soon as a prisoner is charged. Where there are two on-air people in this sort of programme, there must be total trust, cooperation and discipline to ensure that the most immediate diverting of the obscene, the political, the commercial and the illegal is achieved without too much use of the cut-off and the panic button. Robert McLeish, from his immense experience in training within the BBC is clear: 'Very often such a programme succeeds or fails by the personality of the host presenter ... quick thinking with a broad general knowledge, interested in people, well versed in current affairs, wise, witty and by turn genial, sharp and gentle. All this combined with a good radio voice.'[21]

The general principles for a presenter in any other programme apply here too (and probably apply equally stringently to the Christian preacher or pastor!) but they have to be combined with those for a producer. Here, having two people in the studio who are used to working together has proved invaluable. Interchange of views very rapidly at critical points gives stability and assurance to the sound of the programme. Even when everything goes wrong, the panic must not be conveyed to the audience and this is essential to the triangle of trust which gives confidence to those who phone in. Most of the elements of the programme are totally unpredictable and so the shape of the programme, the variety of light and shade, must be constructed as it goes along (what about the liturgy?): music has to be filtered in when needed and done in an appropriate way; calls must be rounded off when they have degenerated to the switch-off of pointlessness to the caller and irritation to the listeners (who are quick to tell us—and why don't congregations?); the balance of the tragic and the light-hearted; the transition across the mountain ranges of the sublime and the mundane; the ability to talk oneself and the audience out of muddles. If the audience felt hesitancy, rudeness, insensitivity, unawareness of wider issues ... the programme would be finished and would never again attain the trust on which it is based. The hypersensitivity to all of this on the part of the audience teaches nightly lessons.

Continuity in presentation is essential in any successful local radio programme. It takes the one-to-one relationship to the ultimate. In other types of counselling, the personality of the counsellor must never become the centre of the stage, but in radio counselling it is the tool which achieves and retains trust: no-one would listen, never mind phone up without it. You don't phone up a thing or a programme, you phone up a person—and you don't phone up a person to be merely handed over to

72

another person or agency. That stage comes once you have achieved the *breakthrough* and the referral has been made possible. Thus, the ideal for the *Open Line* as for any personal situation is that the same people are there every week. If this is impracticable, I believe that at least one of them should be. The occasional counsellor will have a special value and give an extra dimension but can never be part of the centrally identified and trusted dimension.

Another dimension of radio must be borne in mind if we are to get the *Open Line* into proper perspective. It is the well-known fact that talking about things on radio tends to reduce their reality. The remedy in normal programming is the use of actuality. Now the attraction of the *Open Line* to the wider audience is, in my view, not so much the aural voyeurism that is alleged but rather this element of actuality. That is why some people declare that they cannot listen to the programme because it is so disturbing to their emotions: it is too real and people's problems are too real. Some, and audience figures indicate this is the majority, are given hope by realising that others are much worse off than themselves and that even they can be accepted and helped; others are moved to offer themselves to help the needy. The letters received and the immediate on-air offers of help can be quite staggering.

Just to take one example: In June 1989 a man phoned from Glasgow to open out his despair; his wife was in hospital after attempting suicide; he had just learned she was HIV positive; he spoke of his bewilderment and bitterness and his overpowering apprehension about how he could face the future and the responsibility of bringing up four children; he broke down in tears and ended the call. A few minutes later a woman phoned and struggled through her tears to tell the story of her sister who had suffered from HIV infection and then full blown AIDS over the past four years. She spoke to the husband about her nightmare of coming to terms with her sister having AIDS; of the precious times they had had when the infection was in remission; of the demands of caring through the horrors; and of her present searing loss at the death of her sister two days before, a loss lightened only by the loving smile of peace and rest which her sister was able to give her throughout the last few days of her life. She spoke of praying for the man and asked him to remember her. To be in a position to facilitate that bridge of love is at once devastating and humbling: and gives an awesome sense of privilege.

This overwhelming actuality in the *Open Line* is balanced by the element—still retained on this wider stage—that talking about problems reduces them to a copeable size. Thirty page letters are commonplace and after creating an immense sense of helplessness and powerlessness in the reader, they often end with the reflection that the writer feels so much better for having been able to write it all down and that this had only become possible from listening to the programme for weeks or months.

One last point needs emphasis. Counselling on the *Open Line* or on similar radio programmes is radically different from normal counselling (though it may be closer to the counselling required of the priest or minister or Church member). This is one reason why the programme does not necessarily or even normally make use of professional counsellors. They can and have been used successfully when suitable but they have to learn a completely new set of skills. A psychiatrist who worked occasionally on the programme gave clear professional and much appreciated advice to us that this is so. At the end of the day the critical quality will be the ability to broadcast successfully, to establish that one-to-one communication which is free from the barriers of remoteness, irritation and oratory. This is the tool which makes all the rest possible or makes it impossible. We have had excellent professional counsellors on the programme who were rejected very vocally by the audience. Normal professional counselling would be bad radio and therefore bad counselling in the particular radio setting. Additionally, radio reveals who we are with savage cruelty. People have a wonderful acceptance of our shortcomings as persons as long as we are accepting of those shortcomings in ourselves. If we are not, all the counselling or even radio skills we might acquire would never begin to make us acceptable in that triangle of trust that is the *Open Line*. Here again there are surely lessons for the Christian care-er in whatever role.

Breakthrough Counselling

There are many processes and methods of counselling. These can be left aside in the light of the parallel with 'man in the street counselling' and the more specific elements which combine to allow the *Open Line* to be what I have chosen to call *break-*

through radio counselling. Warren A. Jones gives a very simple and useful framework for what has to be done to achieve a real breakthrough to the sort of people who phone *Open Line* or similar programmes:

a)   Achieve contact with the client.
b)   Boil the problem down to its essentials.
c)   Cope actively through an inventory of the caller's ingenuity and resources.

Contact	Focus	Cope
1. Establish the relationship of trust	5. Explore the present situation	7. Inventory of problem solving resources
2. Identify the presenting problem and the precipitating event	6. Identify the threat 'A focus on the factors precipitating the request for help can be therapeutic' (Kalis)	8. Assist in decision making
3. Assist catharsis		9. Emphasise relations with others
4. Build hopeful expectation		10. Summarise new learning[22]

All this can be is an attempt to make a systematised presentation of the sort of factors which have proved essential in working on the *Open Line*: if you like, the application after the event of a rational scheme which seems to make some sense of what happens week by week. It is clear that the whole task of crisis counselling cannot be done and no pretence at attempting to do so would ever be contemplated. That is why it is my view that Breakthrough Counselling is a useful term to describe what the *Open Line* achieves.

The criticism is made that people come out with things that in a later calmer frame of mind they regret. In my view, any damage this might cause is totally offset by the significant therapeutic value of the service we give. It has been experienced time and time again that talking to us as trusted friends, in the anonymity and security of their own loneliness, allows many to make the breakthrough to be able to take full advantage of the anonymous counselling we offer. Having talked abut the problem once, it is reduced in terror to them. Having been accepted by another gives them confidence to go to others on our recommendation (agencies, ministers, doctors etc).

The case of one professional woman stands out. Her son had been convicted of murder and she had read the visiting social worker's file—only to find out that she was blamed in it for the way the lad was. She had been unable over twelve years to talk to anyone because she felt guilty about reading the confidential file. As a result she had the unresolved and accumulated guilt of years, false guilt because in fact she had been an exemplary and long suffering mother (as later emerged). Her letter of a few weeks later said volumes about the breakthrough to further help and peace she had achieved. Only one example of countless, all of which testify to the failure of normal pastoral outreach to pick up so many of the frail suffering ones in our society.

The Religious Element

The religious element has been at the centre of the origins of the programme. In some ways this was purely by chance for the *Open Line*; but perhaps wherever there is a caring Christian community, this is where that community should find itself. It is the sort of service the Churches should be providing if they are supposed to serve Christ in their needy neighbour. From the programme point of view, going to the Churches is a relatively easy way to find properly motivated personnel to add to those whose motivation has different origins. More importantly, any counselling service which ignores the religious support value in a country where almost 90 per cent of the population see it as an element in their lives would be irresponsible. This is particularly true since religion is centred on hope for the hopeless. A counsellor with no religious base would find it difficult to provide the appreciation of a central base of peace and stability which he or she personally sees as delusion. A counselling service based on what was seen as delusion would be a contradiction in terms.

In *Construction of Life and Death*, (1982/1989), Dr Dorothy Rowe—one of Britain's leading psychologists—claims that our beliefs about death and what, if anything, follows it, have a far greater effect on our lives than most people believe, or are prepared to accept:

76

Nowadays, most people will talk about their sex life much more easily than death or religion. Psychiatrists will delve into their patient's sex life in great detail and expound on how it affects their patient's lives. But rarely do they ask the patient to talk about death, the afterlife and religion, except to diagnose the patient as neurotic or psychotic if the patient's views on these subjects do not match the psychiatrist's own views.

Thus she believes that beliefs put patients at odds with the professionals. Death and what follows it are for her the core beliefs for all people and they run their lives, either subconsciously or consciously, to meet the demands that follow from those beliefs.

Death can only be seen in two ways: it is either the total end to life and identity or it is a doorway into another life. If it means a total end to our life, then our purpose is to make the best of our one and only chance at life. If, on the other hand, death is a gateway to another life, then we must live this life to ensure that we gain access to the best possible next life.[23]

This could be a replay of many conversations on *Open Line* with people actively engaged in committing suicide or frightened of being driven to it, or of people mourning loved ones in the Lockerbie or Piper Alpha disasters—or victims either of AIDS or the normal progression of life.

All this is not to say the religionless counsellor is without a particular value but rather to point to the value of the actual religious element we have, provided that the counsellor's personal religious base is never intruded. It can only enter in when challenged by the searching person confronting the counsellor, and it can only be a respectfully presented view of 'what I personally have found helpful'. The naively religious person who sees trusting in God as the simple answer to everything has no place on a counselling programme.

It should be clear from the concept of the programme, but is perhaps worth emphasising, that to use the programme as a platform for a particular point of view would be a betrayal of faith to the station and would have in the past resulted in the supervising Independent Broadcasting Authority taking the programme off air. Explicitly religious questions are often asked—a priceless opportunity for someone with religious convictions—but the following sample of calls from one night's programme shows that in other areas too, the religious insights of Christ are very often crucial elements in the conversation and in the help given:

a woman whose whole family was affected by multiple sclerosis;
a young lad hooked on drugs and in despair;
a husband who wears his wife's clothes;
a man who had lost faith and wanted to pray again;
a man dying of AIDS;
a woman guilty about an abortion years before;
a woman ejected from her house, having been badly beaten up;
a young married man resenting his wife's careful housekeeping;
a homosexual trying to find a way to tell his parents;
a woman worried about a social security offer and her child;
a man having found his wife that evening in bed with someone else;
a schoolboy unable to make friends and ready to commit suicide;
a girl worried about marrying a fiancé she can't really trust;
a schoolgirl frightened by the attentions of a male married schoolteacher;
a widow worried about a relationship to a man with a bedridden wife;
a mother worried about her children's behaviour (lies and stealing).

Again too, a factor which has emerged about the *Open Line* is that as we come to be trusted more, so the number of letters on religious questions has grown. These people find it very hard to talk about things and seem to write with less difficulty. The letters of appreciation afterwards are very moving and worthwhile. The letters on religious questions, however, have their own value, because they give me the opportunity to speak the words of Jesus to those he loved most, the *anawim*, the poor of the earth, the marginalized. One letter almost demands to be mentioned:

I was in a psychiatric hospital for months and had nightmares afterwards because I had been refused absolution after a suicide attempt. I was destroying my husband and two children but your words gave me courage and hope. I went back to confession. When I remember the utter isolation I felt, the sense of having been abandoned—that must be the experience of hell. Your words in the quiet anonymity of the night have given me and my family incredible peace and joy—together again in every sense around the table of the Lord. (Mrs 'Y')

In many ways, the *Open Line* has emerged as one particular and unusual example of what Howard J. Clinebell Jr in *Basic Types of Pastoral Counselling* describes as 'Pastoral Counselling with the Disadvantaged' (.152 ff). He quotes Dale White: 'many of the poor do not express themselves well. They do not see how just talking about it can resolve their problems . . . their concerns are immediate, concrete and pressing. They need to see fast, though limited improvement.' Middle class methods which are client-centred have to be set aside and people contacted where they are.[24] This is at the very heart of local radio and of the *Open Line* contact. The undoubted efficacy of what happens clearly depends on many of the factors in psychiatrist Lewis R. Wolberg's analysis. The persons who phone in can verbalise freely and gain cathartic release from what's troubling them, can rebuild shattered coping mechanisms, can fulfil important needs in the supportive relationship with the counsellor, can lose false guilt by being accepted, can be reinforced by their continued listening to the programme and can be put in touch with supportive groups for further sustaining and growth as opposed to the crisis and stop-gap help the *Open Line* itself offers.

One last aspect of the religious element of *Open Line* should be put on record. It is well illustrated by a letter:

I have long admired the work done by you and Sheila on the radio *Open Line* on Saturday nights. As an octogenarian with hands rather full looking after an eighty-eight year old husband and cottage, there is still *something* I can do for the outer world, I fancy, in prayers for people in sore trouble who consult you. Should you encounter other OAPs who feel 'useless', please tell them this (it is true that age and fatigue sometimes causes me to fall asleep before the close of your marathon programme, but every little helps, I trust).

3

Counselling within Education

VERY OFTEN ideas are implicit in many of the things we do but are not brought to the surface till times of challenge. This was the case for me with the whole massive subject of counselling within education, a multi-faceted reality which can also be approached in a whole variety of ways. For many years I was lecturing in a College of Education, learning as much from the student and qualified teachers I worked with as I was able to impart to them. I was also chaplain in that College of Education and benefitted at every turn from the privilege of being at the centre of the lives of many wonderful people, sisters of the Sacred Heart, lecturers, students and auxiliary staff within the college. This was further enriched by school contacts and work within other non-denominational Colleges of Education.

Parallels in other caring professions became more and more obvious. Thus for example the 'Credo' of the School Nursing Committee of the American Health Association (as far back as 1967 as witness several articles in the American *Journal of School Health* that year)—when discussing how their school nurses are both nurses and teachers—makes it clear that in their role of giving 'a solid core of education for health provided on an individual basis by the counselling process, probably no other teaching technique pays greater immediate and long-range dividends than successful health counselling'. What I found particularly helpful in this is the clear conviction that counselling is an exceptionally effective teaching technique and not just a bland blotting paper role. This prepared the ground, but it was in the midst of controversies about the *Open Line* programme that I was interviewed by Olga Wojtas of *The Times Higher Education Supplement* and her thoughtful questioning crystallised for me a great deal of what I should like to subsume in this chapter under the heading of 'Counselling within Education'.

Counselling in Educational Establishments

Olga Wojtas' article (*The Times Higher Education Supplement* 9.12.88) took us into the realms of counselling in schools and in college and university. Here attitudes have changed over the years but are a long way yet from meeting the needs which prompted the change. Organisations like the Telephone Samaritans report the dramatic increase of loneliness and even suicide among young people and this ranges from primary school to university. Many of the issues outlined at the beginning of this book as demanding a new attitude in the Church and a new attitude from priests, ministers and Christian care-ers have their application or parallel in educational situations: all the issues taken together mean for me that a Christian motivated educational process must take the resulting insights into account.

There are problems of personal identity, problems from broken homes or tortured homes, problems of parental expectations, pressures from competitiveness and the fear of unemployment, problems of drink or drug abuse and factors such as examination pressure which so often get almost inextricably linked with personal problems. In *Prism*, the newsletter of the University of Strathclyde, Dr Shirley Fisher of the psychology department reported in June 1989 that test anxiety affects up to one third of those taking examinations. Between six and four months before the dreaded day, two adverse work patterns may develop. Workaholics (20–30 per cent of students) work for more than fourteen hours a day with no time off. They are subject to bursts of panic and 'are unlikely to achieve maximal use of skills necessary for acquiring a realistic knowledge base'. Workophobics (10–20 per cent) tend to avoid the stress of confronting revision by elaborate avoidance strategies such as staying in bed, creating distractions and many visits home. 'The workophobic is not lazy, but rather is in a high level of anxiety and is effectively immobilised. The phobic response pattern seems to be caused by fear of failure and a high percentage of these students may opt out or even run out of examination rooms on the day, thus protecting themselves from having tried and failed.' Such studies have to be mastered and applied if the counsellor or chaplain is to have the discernment to be helpful.

Primary School

In Scotland, health visitors have done a great deal to help parents understand that primary school can be a frightening place for a lot of young people, but the single class teacher gives a degree of predictable security to the primary school system: team teaching is still in its infancy and is never perhaps so complete as to destroy the security provision of the single teacher. Moves in the direction of team teaching have been compensated for by the schools getting smaller and so to that degree less likely to have frightened little children getting lost in the structures. Nonetheless there can be problems, and the rise in the numbers of children who have to be excluded or have to be sent to special units may well point to the need for counselling to be provided in primary schools and for counselling skills to be built more and more into both initial training and in-service training for primary school teachers.

There are primary school teachers still wedded to a magisterial role which makes discipline easy for the mass of children but severely damages a certain proportion of the more fragile. When the post-war baby boom died away, there were dramatic cuts in the numbers of primary school teachers employed. As a result, today's primary schools have too high a proportion of older teachers—people who are removed by two generations from the television culture which has so changed the discipline and communication patterns effective with the young. Those who consistently resist in-service work tend also to have lost or never acquired the child-centred approach to methodology which with Piaget and Kohlberg has done so much to build into teaching a clear awareness of the limitations of child development both in moral and personal terms. This is damaging in itself for the educational process, but also has the consequence of hindering the changes which see counselling skills as natural to the role of a teacher in the educational development of the child.

Secondary School

The transition from primary to secondary school has now been recognised as a traumatic experience and some measures—unfortunately mainly for performance reasons—have been built into the system to try to compensate. Primary-secondary liaison is a growing area of hard work and the involvement of school chaplains, at least in the denominational schools, is a promising development. If they are sensitive and aware they can give a sense of continuity by their symbolism if not by their previously established relationships and personality.

The provision of Guidance staff in secondary schools was a major breakthrough, spoiled only by the fact that their introduction came first and thoughts of how they should be chosen and trained came very much second. The system is still suffering from that and from problems of where the Guidance system fits into promotion structures. It is still too much a prisoner of old attitudes where the Guidance teacher is often seen as a tool of discipline in the school rather than as an independent person to stand on the side of the pupil against the power structures. On the *Open Line* it has become very clear that some Guidance teachers are fulfilling a vital role for pupils in trouble, and are invaluable bridge people when things are going badly wrong at home and the young people are either not getting the listening ear they need or are actively suffering from what is going on. In other situations, the Guidance teacher has such an image that some pupils would never dream of going to them. That is tragic and perhaps should be a more important part of the evaluation of secondary schools by the Inspectorate and of caring attention by local Churches.

Another issue, which has been troubling many of us, was raised publicly in 1989 when the Brook Advisory Centre—a young people's advisory service throughout Britain—launched a booklet *Confidentiality in Secondary Schools: Ethical and Legal Issues*. It was written in response to concerns that teachers are increasingly expected to take on the role of confidant/e and social worker—for which they receive no training—because of government legislation encouraging more personal contact with pupils. Dilys Went, a director of the centre and senior lecturer in science education at the University of Warwick, is quoted as saying it is the younger, more inexperienced teachers to whom the children most often turn, because they are seen as less threatening: she claims they are least able to cope. 'Intrinsic questions about personal relationships which may arise in the classroom or be asked by individuals, can raise fundamental issues of confidentiality. Teachers, governors, parents and pupils can benefit from a clearly-defined code of practice on confidentiality, which takes into account both ethical and legal considerations.'

Experience on the *Open Line* would confirm that the Brook Advisory Centre report raises important questions on the English scene which have exact parallels on the Scottish scene and this even within the official Guidance system. Chaplains too can get caught in the same trap which emerges from what could be described as a circle of confidentiality, trust and teamwork within the present management of schools. The problem about this is that pupils have to be able to identify who is on whose side. A former murderer who became a minister of the Church spoke very strongly on a *View from Earth* programme a year or two ago, saying that in his view a prison chaplain could not serve both prisoners and warders: having a key to the cell did not come across to the prisoner as the 'sign of trust' it was seen to be by the prison chaplain; instead it identified the chaplain with the 'privileged powers' of oppression.

The parallel in education is not thought about often enough and the young person in trouble is far more sensitive to the 'hail fellow, well met' attitudes of staff and chaplains than most people would credit. When we talk about Christian denominational schools (or Muslim or Jewish schools), an honest detached appraisal would reveal that moral problems of respecting confidentiality and giving space to the pupil to struggle through non-conformist religious or moral attitudes are perhaps even greater than in less homogeneous and less intensely caring educational environments. It is an issue which must be opened up and faced.

Third Level

From the late sixties on, student counselling began to come into tertiary education because colleges and universities began to get worried about high drop-out rates. This has brought much needed improvements but many students still are unaware of the services offered. Even more recently—particularly in the universities of Aberdeen (with much publicised and tragic staff suicides) and Edinburgh (with the appointment of a part-time staff counsellor)—there has been a growing awareness of the requirement for staff counselling. This has begun quite separate from both administration and student counselling and should stay so. As yet, however, many institutions still have no professionally trained counsellor even for students. This problem must be addressed as the pressures of expectations, student loans and fiscal accountability become even greater. Mature students prove to need even more counselling than school leavers.

Two things have emerged as crucial for me. One is that existing counselling services tend to be geared to articulate, middle class clients who are able to package and present their problems. This is not so much caused by the counselling services themselves—but rather by the fact that such people have the confidence and communication skills to know that they can present their problem, and so it is easier for them to overcome the insecurity all of us feel when faced with the thought of presenting our problems to another human being. One of the great values and challenges of the *Open Line* is to be a breakthrough point for the less articulate and give them the confidence to go to the established counselling services. Sad to say, I do not believe that chaplaincy centres are exempt from the problem of being limited in their effectiveness by being too middle class in image and symbol.

The other crucial factor is that in education, the counsellor must be able to bridge the divide between student and officialdom. For this I believe, from my experience as a lecturer and chaplain at Craiglockhart College of Education, that the counsellor must be part of the life of the educational institution. This will mean that the counsellor will be aware of the institutional pressures, aware of the aims and objectives of the institution and the courses within the institution and sensitive to all the currents of thinking and feeling which change so rapidly on the educational scene. The counsellor should be a party to academic decision making though not necessarily a voting participant. On the other side of the fence, the counsellor should be seen by the student to be part of the life of the institution. Contrary to some views on the subject I do not believe this means that the counsellor should join students in the pub. Apart from anything else alcohol will be too high on the list of problems to be dealt with for there to be any doubt about where the counsellor stands on the question of whether alcohol is necessary to academic survival! More importantly, the counsellor has to preserve a degree of separateness: well aware of and relaxed about what's happening in the pub, not seen to be 'other' but consciously perceived as 'different'.

This all means that the counsellor must work hard at having a high profile in the college—though not too high, for that becomes off-putting—and this will have to be achieved in a variety of ways. It should be built into the timetable that every student meets the counsellor soon after coming to college or university: this could be individually or in small groups but must be, while informal, a substantially sufficient contact for the counsellor to be able to sell enough of his or her role and personality to make it easier for the student in trouble to approach him/her. After this initial contact, there should be some sort of reinforcing awareness built into the life of the institution. All this with the proviso that the counsellor like the chaplain must never become identified with the 'power people'.

Lastly, there should be no question of counselling being left only to the designated professional: it should be part of every lecturer's training and remit. This in no way means that they should become experts in psychiatry—quite the contrary. The *Open Line* has taught me the value of 'person in the street' counselling. It is a matter of the listening skills which are part of any good lecturing or tutorial work, being open to the disturbance which probably underlies the academic problem so that the student will get the opportunity to talk about the problem and be informed in the process of where he or she could or should get proper counselling help. The scope for sensitive Christian caring is quite vast and I have been deeply impressed by what so many achieve.

This sensitivity being asked of lecturers is not in my view an additional burden, but rather a consequence not just of human or Christian caring but of good communication skills. Good communication today is seen to begin with the skill of getting yourself across as a person, building a relationship with the person you're dealing with and only then beginning to share knowledge or develop skills. Sadly even now many lecturers, ministers and priests are trained in breathing properly, articulating and projecting their voices but not about the interpersonal elements of communication. If they were, the counselling element would be seen as natural and not as an artificial added extra.

It could well be that the present difficulties in education may lead to a change in attitudes. Lecturers are having to justify much more the work they are doing and there is a lot of self-questioning as a result. We have seen that this can be dangerous, but for me it is another application of the Chinese ideogram for crisis, namely both danger and opportunity.

Chaplaincy

The same is true of chaplaincy in educational institutions. The more secular these establishments become, the more professional they become in services like counselling, and the more education is seen as development from within the student's perceptions and life experience, the more questioning there is about the role of the chaplain. A parallel struck me very forcefully recently when I was doing a programme about the Church's response to the Piper Alpha disaster and the Lockerbie tragedy. (One hundred and sixty seven people died in the fire on the Piper Alpha oil rig in the North Sea in July 1988; at Lockerbie in the Scottish Borders in December 1988, two hundred and seventy died when a Pan Am jumbo jet was brought down by a terrorist bomb.)

At Lockerbie, despite the fact that the team of ministers and priests were by chance on the scene right from the very beginning, there were immediate tensions as soon as the floods of social workers arrived. The chaplains were seen to be nuisances and unprofessional interferers: many felt they were capitalising on human grief and were infringing on the privacy of the bereaved and shocked at a time when they were vulnerable. The problem was resolved at the highest level of the social work provision and good working relationships were established. Yet when, in researching this programme on 'the Church: response to mass bereavement', we turned to the widows, there was a degree of evidence that the Church could come across in a very destructive way.

In Aberdeen, following the Piper Alpha disaster, there were striking witnesses to the differences in approach by the Church people involved: some didn't learn; some learned very quickly; others had a sensitivity from the very beginning which made their caring immensely effective. It struck me from listening to everyone involved that what made the difference was the use of what is described in this book as non-judgmental counselling. In my opinion, the same is true of the chaplain in an educational institution: non-judgmental counselling provides the respect for the individual demanded by the principles of modern education (as well as Christianity!) and provides the setting in which we can communicate all the values, ideals and indeed visions of life which we believe in. This we must explore.

Counselling and Christian Communication

Any book on any aspect of human activity distorts by concentrating on that one human activity. This little book is no exception, so this chapter will attempt to reduce some of the distortion by restoring a little of the context. I believe this is particularly necessary because the type of counselling I have tried to describe—as opposed to systematic professional counselling with all its aims and objectives clearly defined in terms of a specific personality theory—is not so much an artificially devised skill but what we should all do naturally as human beings in the face of people in trouble of one kind or another. It is healthy human communication in those circumstances, which means that education seen as a developmental area of communication for others must in this view of things have a counselling element.

Taking this view of applying the term counselling to large areas of human activity may well be upsetting to those who are professional counsellors, or those who are technically amateur counsellors but whose professionalism in the best sense of the word gives them an invaluable role in society. All I am saying is that what they do so well as a strictly disciplined tool of treatment has to be used also by many professionals and by people in the ordinary pattern of living if we are to be what we should be as caring human beings. I also believe that ministers, priests and Christian care-ers working in the mainstream of parish life should not be counsellors in the technical sense and that what I do on *Open Line* is not counselling in that technical sense either, even though it must follow many of the same rules if it is to avoid doing more damage than good.

Many of course take a different view: thus Clinebell in the line which leads from Dicks, Cabot and Hiltner. This too must be taken into account. My limited view, however, though giving less technical counselling work to priest or minister, paradoxically has the other consequence that the discipline of counselling is seen to be neglected at their peril in the broad sweep of all the work which they do—everything from individual and group relationships with parishioners to teaching, preaching and reconciling. On the model of my broad view of what counselling is, Eugene Kennedy would not let them off the hook. He says:

If, after all our best efforts, we feel that we do not function well as counsellors—and there are people like this—we should

88

at least try to avoid some of our bigger mistakes. And we should not represent ourselves as possessing psychological skills if we find that our personalities keep us from mastering the discipline that is required in good therapists. We can call ourselves advice-givers, philosophers, or whatever, but we must not delude ourselves into claiming that we are counsellors if we are not. Such a decision is much better for ourselves and for those with whom we work. There is no shame in this: we may be involved in education, religious teaching or pastoral work without apologies.[1]

My own view is that no-one should be ordained as a priest or minister, or allowed to teach impressionable young people or engage in pastoral work unless they have made themselves learn the discipline required for counselling. In terms of Christian theology, I believe it is only possible with God's help and gift but this is a clear area of the invitation: 'Ask and you will receive, knock and the door will be opened to you'. We must of course be aware with Paul that 'We are only the earthenware jars that hold this treasure, to make it clear that such an overwhelming power comes from God and not from us.' (2 Cor. 4:7) Or as Eugene Kennedy goes on to conclude: 'For most persons who can learn to listen to others and can employ psychological techniques successfully, the task of being a professional is not an achievement but a never-ending process.'

For a Christian, this is a constant process of listening to God (prayer) and listening to one another, but the guarantee that we can learn to play our part is the wonder of the Incarnation and the mystery of the Church.

Old and new models: Literature Review

In Christian thinking counselling emerges as a consequence of the sort of communication God has chosen to make with the world in the person of Christ and in the group of followers he asked to continue to serve the needs of human beings. In this section I'd like to survey some of the bridging literature between counselling and Christian communication to show that the best thinkers in this area point to the fact that the roots and justification of counselling can be seen also to flow from what is best in human communication in the face of challenge. The literature review will show a coming together of a quite new way of thinking with deep significance for Christian pastoral practice.

David K Switzer in *Breaking Point* puts it well:

> Counselling is acceptance and love of another. It is the facilitation of communication—communication being not just the use of words—even intellectually precise ones—but the art of understanding and being understood. This includes emotional meanings as well as intellectual ones. It is quite clear from this that the counsellor is not merely a detached observer of a process but rather a related participant, albeit more objective than the other person, though not totally objective, since there is no such thing. . . . It is giving one's time, therefore sharing a part of one's life with another, reliving part of his life with him. A counsellor certainly should avoid getting caught in the same emotional trap in which the counselee finds himself, but he does enter into the other person's emotional world with him. The counsellor is a mirror for the other. But he is more than that. He not only reflects feelings, he feels. He not only reflects meaning, he participates in the creation of meaning. . . . All this is to say that counselling is a dynamic personal relationship in which both persons participate and both persons change.[2]

From there Switzer goes on to outline what he considers the factors which make a minister unique as a counsellor. The first in his power as a symbol—very much in the line of Tillich's insights into symbol as the key to the ultimate in being human—and this is far more, of course, than a clerical collar! He represents the community of faith and for some he represents God himself. This has a negative side which has to be worked through for many who have the wrong image of the Church but in positive terms gives an immediate acceptance which others have to struggle to achieve. The second factor making a minister unique is what he describes as the established acceptability for him to take pastoral initiatives in practically every human situation. The third factor is the minister's previous relationships with the people involved. Lastly the minister has unique opportunities as a counsellor because he has the back-up of a community of faith, an immense support personally and a resource to fall back on or organise as back-up to anything that is required.

Another point which I found valuable is his observation that ministerial education in the United States has for many years been based on Dicks, Cabot, and Hiltner, following the principles of Rogers as he progressed in his thinking from non-directive to client-centred counselling; but he notes that it has now begun to concentrate on the particular effectiveness for ministers being involved not so much in long term counselling of whatever kind but rather in short term therapy and crisis intervention. Hence his book and its very fine exploration of the minister's unique power to be helpful when people are at breaking point.

Talking of the change in ministerial education takes me back to another book, namely *The Counselling of Jesus* by Duncan Buchanan.[3] He sets in contradistinction the non-directive counselling of Rogers and the advocacy of directive counselling by Jay Adams in *Competent to Counsel*.[4] Adams sees Nouthetic (admonish, warn, teach) counselling as the only sort which can be said to follow directly in Christ's footsteps. He seeks confrontation with the individual to sort out the things in his or her present situation which God wants to sort out. Buchanan sees his method as short on listening and untrue to the full picture of Christ, whose approach was quite different from starkly calling for repentance as Adams would advise. Possibly, however, he is too kind in noting that this approach is merely open to the abuse of being manipulative: my own feeling is that it is far too open to abuse and attracts the sort of person who is most likely to fall into it. It speaks of aspects of the Christian ministry which should be separated from counselling and which should themselves be 'gentled' by the insights of the appropriateness of the counselling approach.

In other ways, Buchanan's book is helpful. This is true particularly when he speaks of the Jesus of the gospels:

Jesus is neither non-directive, nor directive in the way that the schools of counselling would advocate. He does direct, in a way which is his alone. But he also points people within themselves, to see the true nature of things and comprehend new attitudes. He will not be boxed or put into categories: he breaks out of them with a new way of living and a new way of dying. Life in Christ means moving confidently into each situation, armed only with his authority and motivated only

91

by that which gives glory to God. That is the aim of all counselling: not that we should follow a 'school', or style of counselling, but that we should be the agents whereby people are helped to live confidently in Jesus. . . . Our only aim is the health and well being of the person counselled.[5]

Sister Fran Ferder in *Words Made Flesh* quite deliberately works from both Scripture and psychology to speak of counselling and communication. I feel her insights take our thought yet another stage further. From St Paul, she outlines how caring should express Christian communication. The word it centres on is *'merimnao'* in Greek, a word which means 'caring for' or 'being anxious for'. Thus 'God has arranged the body . . . so that there may not be disagreements inside the body, but that each part may be equally concerned for all the others.' (1 Cor. 12:25) This concern is a mixture of intense feeling for one another and that getting too preoccupied with the wrong things with which Our Lord gently reproached Martha. Christians should quite literally hurt with their hurting and oppressed brothers and sisters. As in the Samaritan story, we ought to 'churn from the bowels' for the needy. The good shepherd looks after the sheep: God cares for everything in nature. Jesus held and touched in the course of healing. Fran Ferder concludes:

> To care for people is to enable them to stand upright. It is to take away the obstacles that weight them down and keep them helpless. It is to relate to them face to face, eye to eye. To talk with them as equals. To touch them with truth and fill them with a sense of worth that spills over into other relationships. It is to stand aside and let them have their glory. Warm people. Concerned people. Affectionate people. Feeling for others. Moving towards them . . . These are the people who speak to us about discipleship and tell us that Christianity is real. They care. They remind us of a God who cares.[6]

Another description I've found helpful is in *Looking out. Looking in* written by Ronald B. Adler and Neil Towne.[7] I feel it will take our thoughts into the practical consequences of the sort of caring and the sort of listening Jesus lived and Paul asked us to imitate. It begins to open out the areas where education and training can improve the quality of our listening.

Adler and Towne first of all distinguish one-way communication—which has little or no feed-back, and is sometimes useful at one-off staged lectures or watching television or allowing someone 'to let off steam' or 'entertain the company with a boring joke'—from two-way communication which is characterised by verbal feedback. For a listener, this means questioning of one kind or another—which can be threatening—or what is called active listening where we paraphrase what the person says to encourage them to open out further and to feel acceptance and caring. Ministers and priests tend to be better trained and more symbolically sympathetic to the other forms of two-way communication which are part and parcel also of their daily work.

Advice, Alder and Towne believe, is fine if you're sure it's correct for those receiving it; that they'll accept the advice; and that they won't end up blaming you if it goes wrong. A judging response is only helpful if it's asked for and if it's constructive rather than a put-down. Analysis, if it's for the listener's benefit and not your own, can help when it's sensitive and guarded. Questions themselves can encourage the person to take a new look at their problem but can lead to digressions or disguise advice. Straightforward support may be fine but may come across as a lack of sympathy or a put-down.

The skill of active listening, with its restatement of the person's thoughts and putting into words for them the often unspoken emotions, is stock in trade for the professional counsellor but, as long as it's not taken to extremes, can be invaluable for priest or minister. A psychologist, Gerard Egan, is quoted in *Looking out. Looking in* as describing several types of active listening (accurate empathetic understanding) which can be summed up in two categories. One is simple reflection—going no further than what the person says—and the other is interpretative reflection. Kahlil Gibran perhaps sums this up nicely when he says: 'The reality of the other person is not in what he reveals to you, but in what he cannot reveal to you. Therefore, if you would understand him, listen not to what he says but rather to what he does not say.'[8]

At the end of the chapter, however, the authors give a salutary warning that active listening should only be used if the problem is complex enough and if the person has the necessary time and concern to carry it through. Undoubtedly what they say is important, but my own feeling is that all of us can learn a great deal for even simple pastoral contacts from reflecting on the technique. I have no doubt from listening in house visits and on the *Open Line* to people who have left the Church, because of what this or that priest or minister said, that all of us have to learn more and more every day of our lives in terms of watching what we say and how we say it in even the most casual everyday contacts. Most of us would be horrified to know what people have taken out of what we said or how we said it—and how it affected them for so many years. I have suffered too with priests and ministers as they reacted to the harm they had done and have seen all too often a growing paralysis arising from that pain or a growing cynicism which makes them care not a whit what they say or who's hurt. Why worry, they say, people will misunderstand you anyway—that's their problem, not mine. Unfortunately, it is a problem for both.

The last book I would like to examine in some detail is Basic *Types of Pastoral Counselling* written by Howard J. Clinebell Jnr.[9] It is a classic in the United States and used widely here in the training of ministers. Clinebell contrasts two models. The older model of pastoral counselling in the forties and fifties, had five characteristics:

1. The formal structured counselling interview.
2. The client centred method.
3. Insight as the main goal.
4. Unconscious aspects of motivation.
5. The childhood roots of adult behaviour.

The new model says that the old approach has made ministers less overdirective but needs to be more flexible and realise that in the everyday life of a minister the structured interview approach is only one of many necessary approaches. It encourages the use of supportive, confrontational, educative, guiding, action-oriented approaches and as a result runs the danger of getting over-complicated and of ending up with a return to the old days 'when I get in a big hurry, I give people instructions, even though I know better'.

Clinebell sees the new model as meeting the historical functions of the pastoral care of the Church. They are healing, which was met by the old model; and sustaining, guiding and reconciling, which he feels were neglected in the old model even

though they have each got counselling aspects. Pastoral counselling he sees as 'a response to the need for someone to really
care for the troubled within the Church fellowship and those
numerous persons who have no Church, but who turn to a
minister for help when crises strike'. Healing he sees historically
expressed by anointing, exorcism, saints, relics and charismatic
healers, but in modern counselling by depth counselling and
spiritual healing. Sustaining was in Church history a matter of
preserving faith, consoling and consolidating and is now reflected
in supportive and crisis counselling. Guiding he sees historically
in advice-giving, devil-craft and listening, and now in educative
counselling, short term decision-making and marriage counselling.
Reconciling is in tradition confession, forgiveness and disciplining,
and this is mirrored in modern counselling by confrontational,
super-ego, marriage and existential counselling leading to reconciliation with God.

One particularly special section of the riches of Clinebell's
book is, for me, the description of the growth of a therapeutic
relationship in counselling. Even from the first session, he believes
a basic rapport should be established and a beginning of the
catharsis of bottled up emotions should be made by listening and
reflecting back the parishioner's feelings. The pastor should
begin to tentatively understand the person's frame of reference,
gain a diagnostic impression, suggest an approach to obtaining
help and if counselling by the minister is to begin, the relationship should be structured.

Later in the book, psychologist Elias H. Porter Jr, describes
five attitudes to be fulfilled by a counsellor's responses. He should
evaluate the person and will in that way imply what the person
might or ought to do. He should interpret in such a way as to
teach the client: this will imply what the person ought to think.
He should be supportive and this reassurance implies that the
person need not feel as he does. He should probe and this very
probing implies that the person ought or might profitably develop
or discuss a point further. Lastly, he should show understanding
which will effectively ask the person to evaluate in response.

What I liked about Clinebell's use of these categories was that
he suggests that all of us pastors, ministers or priests are lopsided
in our pastoral direction by over-emphasising some aspects and
neglecting others. Flexibility in using all of these approaches

95

when appropriate or avoiding others is of me about knowing when to take old or new out of one's store of knowledge in serving others. Examination of conscience for a priest or minister should in my view centre on this rather than on anything else. Pastoral, spiritual and personal formation in seminaries should also concentrate on these characteristics more than anything else and work through the disciplines which professional counsellors take for granted in their training. If we believe that God works in the mystery of our hearts, then the hard work we do in training and in proper in-service retraining must be on the effect ministers or priests have on other people, rather than somewhat fruitless attempts to evaluate the quality of their personal relationship with God. If they give time to God, God will do the rest. Time alone in examining our navels will never begin to help us realise the effect we have one others.

I would have to take exception to one point in this section, however, and that is his stress on keeping records. Whether these are written in the presence of the parishioner or written up afterwards, I feel they can be a destruction of the real and symbolic role that is our great privilege of trust. Other cultures might be different but in our society that sort of approach would destroy our credibility and encourage the wrong sort of detached professional characteristics for any believable ministerial priesthood on behalf of Christ and the community.

Where then do I stand in the debate about the old less interfering model of pastoral counselling and the new more interventionist model? The answer would be that I stand to one side since I am not convinced that priest or minister should themselves engage in structured counselling at all. I do believe that a parish or diocese, deanery or presbytery should set up properly staffed, structured and trained counselling services run by lay people as part of the response of the local parish as a caring community to the needs of the modern world. These world be along the lines of the Catholic Marriage Advisory Service, Lifeline and the still very limited Drug Abuse and AIDS services already established. A service for young people with the independence and approach of the Brook Advisory Centre but with Christian values and ideals would be for me a first priority. For the priests and ministers themselves, however, I believe that the first contacts they make with both parishioners and those with no Church connection should be the non-directive, non-judgmental approach of basic counselling. In the Church of Scotland, two books evidence to the adoption of this sort of thinking. Jean C. Grigor wrote *Grow in Love* as Assistant Director of the Group Relations and Counselling Unit of the Church of Scotland. Her book is a resource for groups and concludes: 'Without love, life is meaningless. The crises of human experience—and special efforts by local congregations—still bring people hopeful of finding acceptance there, back to the Church. If love is not offered and experienced, why should they stay?'[10]

Two ministers in the Kirk's Department of Education, Stewart Matthew and Ken Lawson, broaden this book on group work with a handbook for elders and ministers on pastoral care entitled *Caring for God's People*. It embodies much of the approach advocated in Grigor's book and concludes with a very beautiful passage:

> May we as elders, caring for God's people, learn to be a loving presence with them as we journey and as we sit down with them. A loving presence always involves ourselves, others and God. A loving presence values people. It neither discounts nor rescues them. A loving presence listens to people, with ears and eyes—to the words spoken and unspoken. A loving presence responds appropriately to what it hears, allowing the other person to be responsible for their own life. A loving presence reaches out to the whole of the other person in warm openness and acceptance. A loving presence is open to finding in the other person, a loving presence. To love is to experience God who is love.[11]

Only when this deep initial reverence for the other person has cleared the way to real trust and friendship, can we then by invitation—spoken or unspoken—open out to advise, challenge and communicate the Word of God which has been so badly damaged by our misrepresentations in the past and its associations with division, bigotry and persecution. This whole process can take place in one meeting or it can take a long time, depending on the depth of the wounds in the other person. Christ, I believe, had this initial reverence for the thoughts and feelings of the other person: so also must we.

Preaching and Communication

The attitudes I have tried to draw from others and from my own limited experience of the relationship between counselling and communication have quite enormous implications for preaching and for training for preaching. Because preaching has been associated in the past with the more authoritarian and didactic aspect of the Church, I intend in this subsection to show that a radically new approach to preaching would have to emerge from a proper integration of listening and counselling skills into the Church's understanding of the role of priest, minister or lay assistant in our parishes.

John W.M. Wyngaards in *Communicating the Word of God* sets the scene:

> The authoritarian model of 'Take it or leave it: this is the Word of God' popularly attributed to Jesus, is not reflected in His way of announcing the message. In every situation, Jesus seems to have had His actions and words guided by the needs of the particular people He met. He saw their needs. He took examples from their everyday lives and presented parables that would force them to think. When He was in the company of scribes, He listened to their questions, argued with them and raised questions Himself. When He was with His disciples or other personal friends, He would share their aspirations and worries and make His instructions respond to these. Just as Jesus, the Word of God, was not imposed on mankind from outside, but became one of us, in the same way the word that Jesus spoke was born from His natural relationships with the people: it responded to their needs.[12]

From this Wyngaards goes on to emphasise how we too ought to let our audience speak to us before we can even learn to speak. 'We have to aim at verbalising the questions of the audience in our own words: case histories, questions, confrontations. Experience shows too we may be more out of touch with our audience than we think.' His definition of communicating the Word of God I found useful. It is (i) a verbalised process of learning; (ii) which puts into words people's problems and aspirations; (iii) and which introduces the message from Scripture as an important element in fulfilling the desire or solving the problem; (iv) and which anticipates in words the successful execution of what needs to be done to fulfil the desire or solve the problem; (v) and which anticipates in words the successful execution of what needs to be done to fulfil the desire or solve the problem.

This to me has the right emphasis which will integrate the fruits of modern research in the socio-cultural model of mass communication. He singles out three areas requiring particular sensitivity:

a) The pumping out of a party line (moralising, authoritarian and establishment, uniform, rigidly organisational) as opposed to responding to the real life challenge to freedom and development.

b) Like Isaiah requiring the servant to be careful of the bruised reed, we must be conscious of people at the frayed edges of life. The more specific and the more concrete our presentation is, the more unpredictable and profound it will be. Here he points out that generalisations and abstractions make our communication boring and unreal. In presenting individual persons or events with specific details, we lay a connection with real life. This is applicable in particular to our use of the Bible and the details of real life in which its message is embedded.

c) The re-living of Scripture in our own world must be given high priority. Here he stresses we have to start with the need of people to transcend the limitations of our small human lives. That desire to transcend is the reason for the popularity of the soap operas like Dallas or Dynasty but is ultimately never met adequately by fiction.

Sensitivity is one thing: even more fundamental to communication is the fact that it communicates because it responds to real needs and not imagined ones. With regard to television programming, Dr F.W. Dillinstone speaks of the four great emotional needs which religious television must cater for if it is to be in any way effective. I believe they are just as fundamental for preaching and take us back into the awareness counselling brings to the counsellor. These needs are:

(i) The security of a relationship with one whose care and concern can be relied on.

(ii) The freedom for growth and expansion towards definite fulfillment (surely bringing the exclusion of the narrow patronising or lecturing style that narrows down and imposes perspectives).

99

(iii) The sense of an ordered framework within which life in community can be established in justice and peace (the aim of building bridges in community?).

(iv) The discovery of guidance towards the unfolding of the ultimate meaning of existence (modernised theology, vision and imagination as well as realism and awareness of the transcendent).[13]

Such insights are not new. In *Praise of Folly* (1508) Erasmus is all too modern in his sarcasm about preachers: 'Good Lord, see how wildly they gesticulate; how they vary the pitch of their voices according to circumstances; how melodiously they speak on other occasions; how they sway with their bodies; how they pull a variety of faces; how they fill the whole church with their cries. . . .' After many witty observations Erasmus goes on to say that in the sermon proper they explain a gospel passage but they do this quickly and superficially, whereas in fact this should have been their main task. They then introduce a theological question to impress and the fairy tale to appear witty and clever (their jokes are like an ass playing the lyre). He concludes 'by their ludicrous pomposity and loud-mouthed, ridiculous stupidities they impose a kind of tyranny on the world. And then they imagine themselves preachers like Paul and Anthony of Padua'.

A.M. Roguet gave me unlooked for inspiration from the sermons of the Curé d'Ars. At first, he wrote out his hour-long sermons which were piecemeal concoctions of bits and pieces from the Fathers and the great writers. These he learned off by heart by practising them aloud for hours on end in the sacristy. It was only very much later on that he put aside his copy books and went into the pulpit for catechism and preaching, without any immediate preparation . . . and only then did he come into his own. He had always been convinced of the importance of the word that is preached and many of his words are similar to the emphasis of the Second Vatican Council: 'The divine word is one of the greatest gifts that the good God can give us. I think that a person who does not hear the word of God properly will not be saved. It is altogether impossible to love God and to please Him without being nourished by that Divine Word.' He even says: 'He who listens to the Word of God with a great desire to profit from it is more pleasing to God than one who received Him in communion.' He concluded: 'I only rest twice a

100

day—at the altar and in the pulpit.' He shouted and spoke with poor grammar but:

> Sometimes his face would light up and his expression would be so vivid, especially when he spoke of the love of God, that he no longer seemed to belong to the earth. His speech was simple and artless, but he spoke as a man inspired, with a heart so penetrated and a tone of voice so touching that it was easy to judge from listening to him that a divine fire transported him and lifted him above himself.[14]

At the end of his life he was so worn out and toothless that folk could hardly hear anything. As the Bishop of Belley said in his funeral tribute: 'Even when one did not hear, when one did not understand, the sight of him in the pulpit, merely the sight, preached, touched, converted.' An old parishioner pointed perhaps to one consistent part of his technique: 'All his preaching was by means of comparisons.' This may well link to Christ's use of parables, as expounded by Joachim Jeremias.[15]

Be that as it may, I believe the story of the Curé of Ars, far from being an argument against technique, is a clarion call to preachers today to go through the sort of conversion of technique he went through and then, by rooting their communication in comparisons from real life, begin a more direct type of communication than that ever possible when sermons are either written or over-constructed. It is also a reminder of how the unlikely person can become the instrument of God's word. What counts at the end of the day is commitment. As Robert W. Hovdia put it in *Worship* in 1967, 'If you ask what this has to do with style and presence in celebration, I would answer 'everything—absolutely everything! Commitment, personal commitment, the personal conviction that the gospel and the Church and the sacraments are all together an inseparable and utterly necessary good in the life of man and his world—this is the very first requirement and the fundament of all.'[16] The other foundation is awareness of and respect for the congregation. Fr Alexander Tache is quoted with favor by Raymond Clarke in *Sounds Effective*: 'It is not sufficient for a preacher to be a learned man and a priest, but it is also most important that one should be able to communicate one's knowledge in a manner that is worthy of the Christian message that we are preachers of and respectful of the people who come to hear it.'[17]

Needless to say, whatever we say about preaching must refer back at every point to the preaching of Jesus himself. Fr Brian Connolly in an article 'Preaching: Problems of Communication' has a useful summary:

Christ's technique: power, conviction, authority, mostly He taught seated, out of doors (strong voice, clear communication needed and physically tiring—for our shame) then, direct contact mind to mind, man to man, to learned and to unlettered, concrete not abstract, the particular not the general, his exposition a woven tapestry of pictures not abstract ideas; arguments in comparisons not in syllogisms; he spoke the language of the common man; His vocabulary is from the daily life of His own place and time ... derived from the weather, seasons, nature, crops, animals, birds, occupations, commerce ... His speech patterns are on the familiar level, repetition, question and innumerable easy-to-remember sayings; incidents, people, stories, parables which we who learnt them years go can still remember.'[18]

This must be contrasted with the poor state of preaching in our churches. As Brian Magee put it in *Intercom* in March 1984:

'Some of the faithful are voting with their feet and just not coming. Others have developed a trance-like state not hearing anything, their minds miles away. And priests are known to take the excuse of snow or rain or heat wave to opt out of the task—'I'll let you off with a caution today, we'll just pass round the baskets now.' The young complain of being bored, the homily is irrelevant, unrelated to life. They don't like being talked at rather than to. Priests don't seem to believe what they say, there's no conviction, no communication, as eyes are glued to their text. It all feels too long and monotonous.'[19]

In that same issue of *Intercom*, Patrick Jones is helpful in articulating what a homily should be, when we first listen and then speak. He first quotes from the 1982 statement of the US bishops, *Fulfilled in Your Hearing*:

The preacher represents this community by voicing its concerns, by naming its demons, and thus enabling it to gain some understanding and control of the evil which afflicts it.

102

He represents the Lord by offering the community another word, a word of healing and pardon, of acceptance and love. Like humans everywhere, the people who make up the liturgical assembly are people hungry, sometimes desperately so, for meaning in their lives ... without ultimate meaning, we are ultimately unsatisfied. If we are able to hear a word which gives our lives another level of meaning, which interprets them in relation to God, then our response is to turn to this source of meaning in an attitude of praise and thanksgiving.

This could lead to a wishy-washy sentimentalist homily (if taken the wrong way, and advice like this often is) but on the other hand (if taken in the practical hard-headed style of communication that is the hall mark of the mass media) it could lead to the homily being a powerful bridge between God and the world we live in. The homilist comes for me at the mid-point of the social relations perspective at the point where we have to move into the sort of communication that is a factual reality in the modern world whether we like it or not. In some senses his role must be understood in terms of being another mass medium (and therefore all the rules of being a good broadcaster apply: respect for audience, professionalism, brevity, attention switching, visually effective and personality-centred); in other senses the homilist is an opinion leader: in Katz and Lazarsfeld's sense, this is a role only possible if the homilist is and sees himself as working laterally to his peer group (the only exception being the preacher so old as to be recognisedly older than all his congregation!).[20] At this point, the whole renewed theology of the Church as a circle of equal dependence on Christ (with differentiated function) is vital to enable the preacher to see and live his lateral role. Too many speak as it were from above and too many from what Karl Rahner describes as an 'ivory tower'.[21]

In his *Intercom* article, Patrick Jones also quotes from Ralph Waldo Emerson's Harvard Address 1838:

I once heard a preacher who sorely tempted me to say I would go to the church no more. He had lived in vain. He had not one word intimating that he had laughed or wept, was married or in love, had been commended or cheated, or chagrined. If he ever lived or acted, we were none the wiser for it. The capital secret of his profession, namely to convert life into truth, he had not learned. Not one fact in all his experience, had he yet imported into his doctrine. Not a line did he draw out of real history. The true preacher can always be known by this: that he deals out to people his life—life passed through the fire of thought.

The homilist very often forgets that communication is a bio-social process between himself as a human being and another human being (or one other human being listening with others). The principle in the mass media that the audience is one other human being multiplied by one other, each different but all individual, is vital to be kept in mind by the homilist. Again too the principle that he speaks at this moment and not any other demands of him the impact of actuality which is that of the news, the art of the film that opens frontiers and the social inter-action that is done in the media both by harmless fantasy and sober documentary.

The third helpful quotation used by Patrick Jones is taken from *Sir, we would like to see Jesus*, by Walter J. Burghardt s.j.:

I cannot agree with the cry to give them the dogma, the doctrine, and give it with consummate clarity, with unques-tioning certitude. I grant that many a Catholic is distressingly ignorant of God's revelation, does not know what God took flesh to tell us. Somehow, somewhere, they should learn this. But not ex professo in a homily. The homily, like the liturgy of which it is part and parcel, should proclaim, represent, make effectively present God's wonderful works in the history of salvation: the mystery of Christ should be made present and active within us.

Here too, if the homilist was too conscious of this dimension, he would lose sight of the simple direct inter-personal communi-cation that is imposed on us by the type of communication that is standard in a mass media world and was standard in Christ's own world of personal encounter with the crowds in Palestine, crowds which never seemed to be crowds but gatherings of indi-viduals with their individual needs. Where the dimension of Christ active within us is critical is in the prayer which prepares the service which we give to Christ in the needy and the consciousness that the liturgy is listening to the Word of God, meeting the Word of God incarnate and taking that Word to others in the everyday routine of our lives. John Killinger in *Fundamentals of Preaching* sums up much of the above, especially the first two points:

> Many ministers get into the pulpit and begin to spout sermonic material. Then they get out and it is over. But real preaching grows out of the counselling session, the parish call, the casual encounter in a restaurant or shop. It speaks of and to what the minister has learned in all his dealings with people during the week. It relates the gospel to human situations and works back and forth between them like a weaver's shuttle.[22]

Much of what I have come to believe to be critically important about the sermon/homily I have found summed up in Killinger's book. When it comes to the chapter on constructing a sermon, I believe he ends by getting it all wrong but I'll talk about that later. Other chapters are superb. In writing of the importance of the Bible as rooting preaching in the community and the community's book, his guidelines are clear and helpful. Preaching must be centred on God: a truism but a necessary one. As Karl Barth puts it: 'When people come to us they do not really want to learn more about living: they want to learn more about what is on the further edge of living, God.'[23]

The Bible text has to be studied but then put into context. P.T. Forsyth[24] emphasises that the preacher must rescue the central book of our heritage from 'all biblicist, atomist ideas which reduce it to a religious scrapbook and use it only in verses and phrases'. In restoring life and context to the use of the Bible, the preacher will move away from 'academicitis'. He quotes a great lawyer saying that only twenty per cent of previous careful study should show in a trial, otherwise judge and jury will be turned off. Or as the great preacher Fosdick put it: 'Only the preacher still proceeds upon the idea that folk come to church desperately anxious to discover what happened to the Jebusites.' For me, all of this involves listening to what lies behind the text: God speaking to people and God speaking to us through them.

John Killinger's greatest chapter is on the personal dimension of preaching. Later in the book, he speaks of the person behind the sermon, a person with a balanced life and a balanced range of interests and an acquaintance with all that is happening in society. There's nothing worse to me either than a minister or priest who is so trapped in the petty annoyances of his daily life—the heating system, the sweetie papers dropped in church, the fights in the women's guild or the men's confraternity, the young folk who don't tidy the hall, the football team he follows fanatically, the particular sin he hates in the modern world— that he can see and communicate about nothing else. I had close acquaintance with one such desperately introverted and miserable priest in my own life and have heard of countless others that people have suffered from.

I believe a broad range of reading, cultural interests, news awareness and vision is critical to the preacher as an antidote to that petrifying small-mindedness that can destroy his work—and that work is precisely what John Killinger describes as meeting the personal dimension of the congregation: 'The gospel addresses and assumes the forms of real people's lives or it does not exist at all. It is not theoretical or academic: it is blood and bone, gut and marrow. It speaks to human hurts and hopes, to specific needs and possibilities, or it does not speak at all.' 'The preacher needs to be pastor' said Phillips Brooks 'that he may preach to real men', that is, he or she must move in and get among the people, touching them, hearing them, observing them, in order to preach sermons that contain the gospel for them. He also quotes Henri Nouwen: 'Whenever an answer is given when there is no question, support is offered when there is no need, or an idea is given when there is no desire to know, the only possible effect can be irritation or plain indifference.'[25] More and more I find people reacting week by week with irritation. Killinger is equally convinced: 'The preacher who is really serious about his or her calling should resolve early on never to preach a sermon that does not have the clear and stateable aim of doing something for people.'

In other words we have to preach to people's real needs as we find them walking around and listening to where people are. Edgar Jackson has an interesting study, *How to Preach to People's Needs*. Based on the averages of responses of a congregation's awareness of their own needs, he concludes:

In a congregation of five hundred people, it is reasonable to assume that at least one hundred have been so recently bereaved as to feel an acute sense of loss. Probably a third of the married persons are facing problems of personality adjustment that may weaken or destroy their home life. At least half of the five hundred can be assumed to have problems of emotional adjustment in school, work, home or community that endanger their happiness. Others may have neuroses ranging from alcohol addiction to lesser forms of obsession and anxiety states. Perhaps fifteen or more are homosexually inclined and another twenty-five depressed. Another hundred may be suffering from so great a feeling of guilt or fear of discovery that their peace of mind and health are jeopardised. The rare individual with complete peace of mind and soul is probably surrounded by those who are carrying several heavy burdens within.'[26]

In my own life I know I only began to preach properly after I had experienced that sort of survey in my own work. The ultimate tragedy for me is the preacher who seems not to see such reality or at least not relate it to the rest of his life and work (perhaps in a self-preservation instinct?). Fred Craddock[27] notes that this involves a change of technique: from the deductive (principle through to application), to the inductive (situation/ need through to truth which can help). Within a few sentences, the congregation should begin to recognise that the preacher is talking of something that is vital to them: and this will show on their faces! If there isn't that response, the preacher must abandon what he's doing and try again. Fosdick again in 1928 in Harper's Magazine:

The mediocre sermon produces an effect of emptiness and futility largely because it establishes no connection with the real interests of the congregation. It takes for granted in the minds of the people ways of thinking that are not theirs, and in consequence uses a method of approach which does not function. It is pathetic to observe the number of preachers who commonly on Sunday speak religious pieces in the pulpit, utterly failing to establish real contact with the thinking or practical interests of their auditors.

It is at this point that the whole theology of story enters in. As Frederick Buechner wrote:

107

At its heart most theology, like most fiction, is essentially autobiography. Aquinas, Calvin, Barth, Tillich—working out their systems in their own ways and in their own language—are all telling us the stories of their lives, and if you press them hard enough, even at their most cerebral and forbidding, you find an experience of flesh and blood, a human face smiling or frowning or weeping or covering its eyes before something that happened once.[28]

It's these stories we have to preach. We can even use our own stories though I was glad to see Killinger emphasise these should be of our weakness together rather than self-centred stories which put the preacher in a favourable light. I know one congregation which emerges every Sunday groaning at the self-centred stories of the priest, especially since they go on for ever and interrupt the liturgy not just once in the homily but intermittently.

Killinger is also excellent on the necessity of integrating the insights of modern psychology with our 'life learning', while warning of the dangers of preaching self-help therapy rather than God-centred faith. I'd like to add two other quotations he uses. The first is a warning from David Switzer not to pick up on a particular problem area, label it and then give some Christian answers to it.

When such an approach slides over into an easy palliative inspired sermon, it often does not communicate to persons the depth and complexity and conflicting nature of human emotion and experiences which comprise the reality of their lives, and even though some may like the sermon, it does not lead them into the experience of being understood, and thereby not into the difficult process of self-exploration which is the prior and essential condition for effective decision-making and change.[29]

His model is parallel with the counselling process. In both, the aim is to lead people from self-exploration to goal-setting to evaluation of alternatives to decision-making to action to self-exploration again and so on.

The second quotation is again from Harry Emerson Fosdick. He says there are four things to be done in a sermon:
(i) To identify a pressing human problem and gain each hearer's personal interest in it.

(ii) To develop understanding of the problem in terms of common solutions people have tried, usually without success.

(iii) To set the problem in the biblical perspective and to secure the hearer's cooperation in discovering how much richer and more satisfying that perspective is than any other.

(iv) To encourage the hearer to accept and act on the biblical answer to his or her problem, thus mastering the problem and preparing to meet life at a higher level.

It is when John Killinger begins to speak of constructing the sermon that I begin to disagree with him. He speaks of Bishop James Pike of California as having a disturbingly casual approach to preaching. Pike said he gave some thought to sermon material on Saturday night, consulted a few commentaries and 'formed a kind of outline' in his mind. He reflected on the outline after going to bed and again in the morning. Then he went into the pulpit and preached without any notes at all. His argument was that the preacher who does not write out a manuscript uses oral language, whereas the one who writes becomes high-flown and difficult to understand. I myself would add literary and in such a person to person medium totally non-communicative.

My pattern now is that of Bishop Pike but—as I suspect he would—I would maintain that all I do, pastorally, intellectually, casually, and above all in counselling, is my preparation for each sermon: and that is hard work and work that is highly structured by means of the objective that I have to build bridges between God and man and man with man. It's true that I began by writing and reading sermons; progressed to writing and not reading sermons; then to writing bits and an outline; and then to writing very little of anything. It may well be that this is a necessary progression but I believe it is the last two stages which should count as the standard way of preparing a sermon. I believe that it is a longer journey and one demanding much more professional expertise to read a longer sermon and make it real communication than it is to achieve real communication of what is only in written or mental outline. On one national occasion recently I groaned through a forty minute episcopal exercise in literary construction that never left the bishop's desk at home to become real communication in any sense of the word. I prayed for a wind to blow away the sheets of paper and that he might speak as he was no doubt capable of speaking. I also wondered whether he glanced at any stage at the congregation, for I was sure that if he did he could not have continued with his script.

Having said all this with a certain hesitancy, I am now going to commend a great deal of Killenger's work on constructing a sermon. I think anyone attempting to preach should know (like learning to drive a car) the mechanics and the theory of construction before letting it disappear into the learned craftsmanship of actual communication. He joins many in suggesting that the preparation for the next Sunday begins on the Monday morning before. In a sense I agree, but if you're preaching every day you can use up your idea during the week before and be left with nothing for the Sunday. This will be particularly true on those irritating occasions when a Scripture reading occurs twice in a short period, for I believe firmly that what is said in a homily should be new to the preacher at least in some vital aspect—or he should say nothing.

The search for something new (as well as old) may be easier if it has scope all week but in practice I find that a live congregation only becomes real when they are about to materialise. Six days beforehand they are an identikit, theoretical, even though you have just addressed them the day before. Their thoughts and concerns will be shaped by the news and events of the week, nationally, internationally and individually. However, W.E. Sangster chose his themes ten days in advance and worked on them for ten days! George Buttrick spent a minimum of twenty five to thirty hours on each sermon! Paul Scherer forty hours! They raise vital questions for much of our preparation.

Where I agree totally with Killinger is that the critical point (whether the night before or the week before) comes after assembling at random the ideas available either by brainstorming or from a preacher's notebook that is gathered day by day. That point is the writing of a sentence which will sum up concisely what you wish to say. This is a principle of broadcasting and a principle of counselling. In educational phraseology, it is the objective i.e. the precise information, emotion, development etc. that, in the light of your aim in preaching, you wish your congregation to have retained from your communication. All the material about Bloom's taxonomy of educational objectives and the definitions of objectives is relevant and helpful here. 'No sermon' said John Henry Jowett 'is ready for preaching, nor ready for writing out, until we can express its theme in a short, pregnant sentence as clear as crystal. I find the getting of that sentence is the hardest, the most exacting and the most fruitful labour in my study.'[30]

To be fair to Killinger, I must return before concluding to another section of his outline of techniques when he quotes John Redhead of Greensboro, North Carolina: 'paper is said to be a poor conductor for heat'. This of course is my view and is for me the inevitable consequence of applying to this sphere the personal sensitivity of the communication which takes place in counselling.

The famous preacher Fosdick abandoned extemporising in later life in favour of reading. He believed he was still able to make to person contact; but Edmund Holt Linn, who studied his preaching, concluded that the process did not leave him as free, spontaneous and direct as he liked to believe he was. If such an expert failed, so much more in my view is it out of the question for the learner. I repeat again: it takes incomparably more skill to write the spoken word and then lift it off the page than it does to speak what is in one's heart.

Killinger concludes by suggesting that one should preach naturally, preach animatedly, and preach responsively. My only quarrel here is with the 'animatedly': if animation or liveliness is natural it is what it should be, but if it is forced, as it often is, it is worse than counter-productive! To preach responsively is to apply to preaching everything I have tried to say about counselling. I would feel even more strongly than he does that if one has to be responsive and natural one must speak extemporaneously. I have often gone into a service and scrapped a whole sermon in favour of another, precisely because I felt that the first was not right for that particular congregation in the particular mood they were in that day. At other times I've changed course radically half way through. I don't believe there's any way you can know what's right till you feel the vibrations coming back in the actual service. It's these sort of skills that training for preaching must develop and that an educated laity must demand from those who dare preach to them. It is their right to expect it in return for supporting their priest or minister in his privileged role in the community. To see their preacher as first a listening counsellor and only then as the exponent of God's Word will change the expectations of the laity about their pastors, and establish proper sensitivity in the new ministers at the very beginning of their trying to take a full part in the life of the Church.

I'll leave the final word to Colin Morris. From the principles of television, he draws similar conclusions for the sermon to those I feel will follow from a pastor who learns from his counselling approach the approach he should take to the people he tries to serve:

> The electronic media have tutored a whole generation to get the point of information quickly, so the attention span has contracted. The thirty second commercial, the three minute news report, the ten minute variety act: these make limited claims on the viewer's attention whereas previous generations were attuned to the forty five minute lecture, the fifty minute classroom lesson and the thirty minute sermon. Though the faithful love the exquisitely slow build-up to a totally predictable conclusion, those outside the charmed circle find the sermon a very laboured way of communicating information.[31]

Christian Counselling and Religious Education

The Application of Counselling Skills to the Role of Parent, Teacher and Pastor

To see Christian counselling as the practical embodiment of the attitude which follows naturally from Christ's approach to people is paralleled directly in the latest theories of religious education and the spiritual and psychological insights which have now become normal in recommendations for parents, teachers and pastors in their approach to the young. Many books could be devoted to the subject. The research of Piaget, Kohlberg and Fowler have established the limitations of children's and young people's ability to have the necessary concepts for religious and moral decisions. A better understanding of how moral development takes place means that the nature of education has had to change and simplistic attitudes and aims have been seen to cause serious damage to moral development.

The influence of the mass media too has changed the nature of the learning environment: children are presented from the earliest age with a variety of stimuli and a wide range of values. Even parents who claim to limit and monitor what they see have to contend with the fact that the most powerful element in the influence of the mass media is 'by peer interaction', that is by peer groups talking with one another about what they have seen or not seen on television. The effects of all this range from 'slap-happy' parents having to question whether they can force their children to behave, to deep questions about how parents should react to the searchings and alternative thinking of their 'young atheists', some as young as seven!

Rather than holding our hands high in horror, which would do no good, we must face the challenge of helping them, become conscious of their dependence on their environment—both that of their parents and that of the media world—and setting them free to allow the Christian life to become a significant option. This combines with the growing awareness of how difficult is it to make real the 'Christocentricity' of all religious education, such as is described by the Second Vatican Council. A learning environment tied in to the visual and dependent on the current scientific theory that what cannot be measured does not exist raises again the challenge to parents, teachers, ministers, priests, and Christian care-ers to make Christ real for the young in their own caring relationships.

Parents 'are to be acknowledged as the first and primary edu-cators of their children' was the unequivocal statement which emerged from the Second Vatican Council.[32] This has helped to raise their status but growing problems of communication between parents and children have made their task more dif-ficult. It is a mixed situation. The sort of problems being talked about between parents and young people are: lack of under-standing, affection and agreed sexual guidelines; drink and drugs (on both sides); 'home is where the hatred is'; alienation ('I built walls . . .'); a sense of injustice leading to suicide; the pressure of values in the media; perceived lack of sincerity in parents, teachers and pastors doing their 'God thing'; a perceived con-veyor belt religious education with lists of dos and don'ts. The sorts of answers talked about are realising the 'child is the father of the man': parents spending time with their children (as op-posed to letting TV be the child-minder); renewing the support of the extended family; encouraging parents, teachers and pastors to show more caring; new more child-centred methods of religious education; greater cooperation of parents and teachers

113

in school. One lecturer for whom I have a great respect uses the acronym PARENT to highlight patience, articulation, respect, encouragement, nurture and tolerance. I would add the qualities of listening, being patient, being positive and being friends. It's not too difficult to see the same qualities emerging from religious education theory as emerge from the counselling perspective.

An example in Fran Ferder's *Words Made Flesh*[33] illustrates very clearly how the right approach from a parent can help enormously but the wrong approach can be desperately damaging. It's a letter a young girl Kate received from her father:

> You have your mother and I very upset. We haven't slept good for weeks and my ulcer has been acting up. [Makes her feel guilty]
>
> Everytime I think about what you are doing I wonder where we went wrong. [manipulating martyr behaviour]
>
> Going with that divorced man is going to ruin the whole family. [a brutal attack of blame]
>
> Kate, he's not for you. In the eyes of the Church he's married. [unasked for advice causing resentment]
>
> He's probably talked you into believing it's all OK and that we're just old fashioned. [unfair assumption and judgment]
>
> You're always together. You can't tell me that nothing will come of it, or that it's all innocent. [accusation charged with suspicion]
>
> If you love us, you'll take my advice. [a bribe and a test]
>
> Mother and I love you very much. [an expression of love after such an attack comes across as unloving and a conscience salving exercise]

Similar letters abound on the *Open Line* or are complained about on it in call after call from distraught young people. After counselling of Kate and her parents, the rewritten letter read like this:

> I have been upset and angry lately, and I need to talk abut it with you. It is hard for me to understand your relationship with Tom since he is divorced. He does seem like a fine fellow, and I want you to know that I do like him. However, the thought of my special daughter going out with a man who is still married in the eyes of the Church is a hard one for me to

swallow. I just wanted you to know that I know you will do what's best. I want very much to understand, so let's keep talking about it. You are an adult and whatever you decide to do I will always love you.

This is communication and this for me is an example of that application of counselling skills to the role of parent, teacher and pastor which is called for at every age and in every situation of formal and informal religious development. In time there comes the clash between parents and children's non-practice. The parents shouldn't shrug it off of course but should understand that most often their children's non-practice is a reaction against an accepted way of life. This needs restraint and hard work. They shouldn't give way to the temptation of saying 'We had difficulties but we didn't stop going', because in one way or the other they'll get the response 'You were never my age—at least in this day and age.' Karl Rahner's theological insights are often helpful at this point to reinforce the instinctive counselling approach. 'It's not faith that has changed. What has disappeared is a whole cluster of pre-conditions for the special faith found in a traditional society.'[34]

From studying relationships it becomes clear that parents tend to use the language of doctrine and obedience rather than what would be more helpful and in line with modern catechetical thinking, namely the language of shared experience. When young people complain that services are boring, they're generally right but they can be challenged as to what they bring to the service! They speak of hypocrisy and though sometimes they are right, more often they need to develop the listening ear of the counsellor to appreciate that those they think hypocritical are just as mixed up as they are but are hiding behind barriers of confidence and convention. The aim for parents should be achieving communication rather than conformity and they must not be put off by aggressive pronouncements, silence or 'deafness' for these are just very natural protective devices. Once again we come back to Our Lord's attitude with the woman at the well. He stayed with her and was in no way put off by her aggressiveness, her changes of mood or her defensiveness. So must we stay with our young people—and the door is opened for them to real religious and personal development.

Within formal education, both the modern concept of the nature and justification of the Catholic school and the new theories of religious education underline the necessity of an open-ended counselling approach. The Catholic school is seen as a community of faith in which what is taught and then experienced in meetings with Christ has to be matched by the living out of faith, the encouragement of a response to the same challenge that faces educator and educated alike. It is to be a caring community within and an outreach to the needs of the community around: and part of that caring outreach is dialogue with and respect for others whose values and attitudes may and indeed will contradict our own in many aspects. All of this means listening within and listening to those outside, as well as listening to God at the heart of all our searchings.

The insights of the educational psychologists reinforce the necessity for respect and patient listening within the community of searchers that is the Catholic school (and the parish community of course which is either a partner with the school in this educational work or may have to substitute for its role in addition to its own if there is no Catholic school). Piaget warns that a child's concepts of what is right and wrong begin by being based on the material damage caused by their actions. The educational process can either reinforce this or allow the child to develop to a higher stage of morality. The classic situation is the sort of day to day happening where in the home, for example, Auntie Jean (strict, old-fashioned) is coming to tea. The children are warned to be on their best behaviour, the best china is out, the best teacloth. At first all goes well. The first crisis is overcome when wee Johnny (who is one of those little chaps who get away with murder because they're funny with it!) was really cheeky: silence fell but Aunt Jean laughed so all was well. At tea, however, Johnny accidentally knocked over the jug of milk—over the table and over Aunt Jean's dress. Needless to say he was punished for this! A trivial incident, you might say, but Johnny had had reinforced the material damage criterion and had not been encouraged to see that his being deliberately impertinent and hurting was far more wrong than an accident: he was responsible for the one but not for the other, yet what he was not responsible for was taught as being morally wrong.

Piaget's second stage of moral development depends on the social approval or disapproval of others. True morality for him only begins to come in when the child is capable of abstract concepts and this is when the child is very much older than Christians in the past have presumed. Kohlberg and Fowler take this very much further until we are faced with the position that adults are far less capable of full responsibility for moral decisions than confessors in the past ever imagined. In parallel with this, Goldman and those who followed him have shown that we must be very careful about both childhood and adult ability to comprehend the whole range of biblical and religious thought.[35] Now in all these areas there are major reservations which can be made about their conclusions, but they do undermine the old presumptions and they do provide unquestionable foundation for pastors having to avoid judging on appearances and instead listening in such a way as to allow the real person to emerge from the confusion of good, bad and indifferent which is for most of us the most accurate description of our inner reality.

The theology of story has given birth to a 'catechetics of story' with educators like Paolo Freire.[36] In place of 'telling people the unchangeable truth' and 'telling them they're all wrong' it is suggested that the more effective way to teach the truth and help people to understand the attractiveness of right rather than wrong is to share the story of our faith. It is a matter of bringing together into constructive dialogue the educator's personal story of faith, the student's own story of faith, the story of faith of the 'cloud of witnesses' who have gone before us in the faith and of course the story of the faith of Jesus and those he gathered round him to learn and communicate the faith to those who would come after.

The American catechetical approach, which takes its name from the Rite of Christian Initiation of Adults and follows a particular group approach to that rite in every area of Christian education, presumes that the sharing of our stories of faith can best be done by Christians spontaneously baring their souls with one another in groups. In my opinion, this attempts what is invaluable in person-to-person counselling in the group context without the safeguard of confidentiality and training in the counsellor to protect that unfolding. It has parallels in the movement for family, parish and group counselling which has mushroomed within and outside religious circles, but it attempts to do similar

117

things without trained leaders, clear objectives and a psychological theory to underpin the discipline of the group situation.

There are immense possibilities for such healing, educational and spiritual development counselling in the future, and the Church of Scotland has done much pioneering work in this direction. To attempt, however, to mimic the good effects without a careful structure, leaving the interaction to become fruitful by the intervention of the Holy Spirit is to get things the wrong way round, and to forget that while everything depends on the Holy Spirit the Incarnation demands that we get on with the hard routine work ourselves with all our human effort and insight. We are to be like the wise virgins who took oil in their lamps and didn't just presume God or somebody else would provide! While—like counselling—RCIA and similar soul-baring can have immensely liberating effects, my own view (from trying to patch up the casualties of such groups, who afterwards had good reason to regret bitterly what in the emotion of the group they had shared) leads me to feel the approach takes a good thing too far. Others would disagree, but I feel that the holders of both views would benefit from reflecting on how much of the sensitivity of counselling is involved in what is being done and how necessary it is to be aware of the dangers as well as the possibilities in what is being opened up. Both group and individual sharing point to what I have tried to outline in this little book as a somewhat neglected aspect of Christian caring. The multitude of possible incarnations of this for Christian individuals and groups alike lies outside my intention and competence: I hope I have made the principle clear. I'd like to finish this section with the concluding remarks of Fran Ferder In *Words Made Flesh*:[37]

> As followers of the Lover from Nazareth, friendship is our heritage. Building relationships is our call. Effective communication is foundational to our call. It prepares us to listen with our ears and to hear with our hearts. It fills us with longing to gather people in our arms as a hen would her chicks. It enables us to find a compassion powerful enough for outcasts and big enough for ourselves. It readies us to put down stones so we won't hurt even the sinners. It gives us words made flesh.

4

Christ the Counsellor

The Suffering Servant

BEFORE THE BIRTH of Christ, there was a range of ideas among the Jewish people as to how God's promised 'Messiah' would bring about the salvation they longed for. The one which hit the headlines, as it were, was the political Messiah, a king who would lead them to a military victory that would begin for them the sort of world dominion then enjoyed by the Romans: that dominion would bring salvation. Smaller groups, however, were looking for a spiritual leader who would establish God's kingdom in a quite different way. As a result, there was a body of material already existing in the Jewish scriptures about the expected Saviour which the early Church could make use of to teach about the Jesus whom they were convinced was 'Good News' for all mankind. One of the sources we know most about in this process is the set of poems about the Suffering Servant. These are found in the later sections of the writings attributed to Isaiah in his successive incarnations in a series of prophets in the great prophetic tradition he established.

In the first song of the servant of Yahweh we read about the servant:

He does not cry out or shout aloud,
or make his voice heard in the streets.
He does not break the crushed reed,
nor quench the wavering flame. (Is. 42:2–4)

The contrast is made between the servant and political powers like Cyrus in dealing with the afflicted and the weak. Our Lord chides his disciples very much in the spirit of this verse: 'You know that among the pagans the rulers lord it over them, and their great men make their authority felt. This is not to happen among you. No; anyone who wants to be great among you must

119

be your servant, and anyone who wants to be first among you must be your slave, just as the Son of Man came not to be served but to serve, and to give his life as a ransom for many.' (Mt. 20:25–28). There is no evidence of Jesus roaring at people to conform but plenty of evidence of him—in the spirit of Isaiah's poem—seeking out and serving the crushed reeds, the wavering flames. These crushed reeds and wavering flames might be far from meek and mild: they might well be argumentative, stubborn and convinced that they are right and Jesus is wrong, but his gentleness remains.

The second song of the servant of Yahweh speaks of how sensitivity to the crushed reed and wavering flame—non-judgmental counselling if you like—does not exclude speaking the truth.

> He made my mouth a sharp sword,
> and hid me in the shadow of his hand.
> He made me into a sharpened arrow,
> and concealed me in his quiver. (Is. 49:2)

God gives the words and the protective love that is necessary to support the one who speaks his message. In fact, he sets the servant aside: he pronounces his name, that is he sets him aside for his special task. 'You are my servant, in whom I shall be glorified' (Is. 49:3); and yet the servant feels himself to be toiling in vain, exhausting himself for nothing—a picture which for the early Christians, applying this to Christ, will square with him looking over Jerusalem and weeping because they had not been able to respond to his message.

What is being suggested by the poem and its application is the context for speaking the truth, namely service of the needs of others; and this speaking is to be done from within humanity and through humanity. This is the terrible tension Jesus endured: between a very real sense of frustration and failure and a deep trust in God. It is fascinating to analyse the times in the Gospel when Jesus speaks out and the times when he is silent. We will return to this later. In terms of the canticle, the challenge for Christ, and derivatively for us, is that the Lord 'has made my mouth a sharp sword...' the double-edged sword of the Word of God which is to be pictured in the New Testament as cutting to the quick. This image, however, is immediately tempered by another. He has been made into a 'sharpened arrow' alright but God, he says, has 'concealed me in his quiver' until the opportune moment. At that opportune moment—but not before—Our Lord says we should speak straightforwardly (a yes for a yes and a no for a no) and incisively.

Fr Raymond Brown in *Priest and Bishop* points out that many preachers today are willing to confront their people on the level of social and political evils but unwilling to confront them on matters of doctrine and personal morality. He has to admit, however, that in the past we have been too keen to label actions as sinful and too ready to damn legitimate theological differences. The principle of correction is a Christian one—if it is done with love and out of love and never erected into an institutional monstrosity like the Inquisition or the 'Chapter of Faults and Discipline' in religious life. St Paul in 2 Cor.12 is a good example of what he learned from Christ. He had to speak frankly and reproachfully but then ask very humanly 'Because I love you more, must I be loved the less?' Paul, in following Christ, was prepared to lose his 'popularity' for speaking out but regretted having to do it. Speaking out can only be done when like Paul we are 'perfectly willing to spend what I have, and to be expended in the interests of your souls'. Again too—as Karl Rahner points out—any apostle or priest is a man who prefers to be silent, who has great need of 'parousia'. This is not so much boldness as 'the courage of one's convictions, a certain courageous and optimistic outspokenness'.[1] This the early Church saw to be characteristic of the Christ they worshipped.

The third song of the servant of Yahweh is central to the picture of the servant which the early Church found so apt for describing Christ. The listening that is the central theme of this book is made crystal clear: listening to God in prayer and then being able to listen to others:

The Lord Yahweh had given me
a disciple's tongue.
So that I may know how to reply to the wearied
he provides me with speech.
Each morning he wakes me to hear,
to listen like a disciple.
The Lord Yahweh has opened my ear. (Is. 50:4–5)

121

To see this in Christ is a mixture of reflecting on his nights of prayer on the mountain before his major decisions and his prayer in the garden of Gethsemane, and examining carefully the way in which he listened to individuals. His choice of the parable as a teaching method is also critical to any appraisal of his humanity at work. His dealings with 'the wearied' are where we find the clearest evidence of his prayerful listening.

It is helpful to look at modern spirituality to reflect on what Christ has inspired in others because of what he was in himself. Cardinal Garonne for example suggests that 'in our world, silence is being lost. It is prized less and less. Some even claim it is devoid of value. In any event there is a rush to avoid it . . . it is one of the profound values of Christian life.'[2] Ladislaus Boros names the ability to fall silent as 'one of the main bases of the Christian hope'. Only in silence can we hear God saying 'Take heart, you are not alone.'[3] Louis Evely has a good metaphor: silent prayer is to change gear and let God's power take over and drive us on.[4] This change in us by listening to God in prayer is expressed very well on a practical level by Bonhoeffer:

> I can no longer condemn or hate a brother for whom I pray . . . no matter how much trouble he causes me. His face, that hitherto may have been strange and intolerable to me, is transformed in intercession into the countenance of a brother for whom Christ died, the face of a forgiven sinner. Everything in him that repels us falls away and we see him in all his destitution and need.[5]

Or again Michel Quoist: 'If we knew how to listen to God, we should hear him speaking to us—through his Word and through life.' And: 'If we knew (through prayer) how to look at life through God's eyes, we should see it as innumerable tokens of the love of the Creator seeking the love of his creatures. The Father has put us into the world not to walk through it with lowered eyes, but to search for Him through things, events, people.'[6]

Clearly, there is a danger in projecting back speculatively into Christ's inner life, but the insights of all these writers—taken together—mean to me that, if we are to give full justice to his humanity, we must surely begin with Christ's ability to fall silent and listen: first to God his Father and then to his fellow human beings. This is a new approach in theology and a significant one for the argument of this book that the counselling approach is a specifically Christian approach.

The fourth song of the servant of Yahweh (Is. 52:13–15; 53:1–12) opens out for the first time what is to be the inner paradox of Christianity, the contrast between glory and suffering. It begins and ends with glory—but as for the bit in between! And yet that 'bit in between' is a very powerful description of the situation of so many people—a situation to which Christian counselling has to respond. It is also the qualification which enables Christ to be the counsellor, namely the fact that he himself has experienced suffering.

> See my servant will prosper,
> he shall be lifted up, exalted, rise to great heights.
>
> As the crowds were appalled on seeing him
> —so disfigured did he look
> that he seemed no longer human—
> so will the crowds be astonished at him,
> and kings stand speechless before him;
> for they shall see something never told
> and witness something never heard before:
> 'Who could believe what we have heard,
> and to whom has the power of Yahweh been revealed?'
> Like a sapling he grew up in front of us,
> Like a root in arid ground.
> Without beauty, without majesty (we saw him),
> no looks to attract our eyes;
> a thing despised and rejected by men,
> a man of sorrows and familiar with suffering,
> a man to make people screen their faces;
> he was despised and we took no account of him.
>
> And yet ours were the sufferings he bore,
> ours the sorrows he carried.
> But we, we thought of him as someone punished,
> struck by God, and brought low.
> Yet he was pierced through for our faults,
> crushed for our sins.
> On him lies a punishment that brings us peace,
> and through his wounds we are healed.

We had all gone astray like sheep,
each taking his own way,
And Yahweh burdened him
with the sins of all of us.
Harshly dealt with, he bore it humbly,
he never opened his mouth,
like a lamb that is led to the slaughter house,
like a sheep that is dumb before its shearers
never opening its mouth.

By force and by law he was taken;
would anyone plead his cause?
yes, he was torn away from the land of the living;
for our faults struck down in death.
They gave him a grave with the wicked,
a tomb with the rich,
though he had done no wrong
and there had been no perjury in his mouth.
Yahweh has been pleased to crush him with suffering.
If he offers his life in atonement,
he shall see his heirs, he shall have a long life
and through him what Yahweh wishes will be done.

His soul's anguish over
he shall see the light and be content.
By his sufferings shall my servant justify many,
taking their faults on himself.

Hence I will grant whole hordes for his tribute,
he shall divide the spoil with the mighty,
for surrendering himself to death
and letting himself be taken for a sinner,
while he was bearing the faults of many
and praying all the time for sinners. (Is, 52:13–15; 53:1–12)

The fourth song of the servant also introduces the unheard-of mystery that still baffles our theology: ours were the sins Christ carried, ours were the sufferings he endured. But what does that mean for us today in an age where the medieval, rather masochistic overtones of vicarious suffering have been surpassed and seen to be inadequate? In a discussion in the early seventies between the Faith and Order Commission of the World Council

124

of Churches and the Vatican Secretariat for Promoting Christian Unity, they were trying to isolate the characteristics of a Pauline apostle. A Protestant minister surprised many by suggesting that suffering was one of the most distinctive characteristics of the Pauline apostle—not preaching but suffering! Fr Raymond Brown in *Priest and Bishop* found himself in full agreement.[7] Alan Paton, referring to Gethsemane, stresses the same characteristic of the servant of God in this world.[8]

These authors reflect the fact that the early Church clearly used the fourth song of the servant to present Christ in this way. As such it lays the theological foundation for seeing Christ as the 'empathizer', the sufferer with and for, the counsellor. Christ fulfilled the canticle and has made it clear that to be his disciples, we must take up our cross and follow him—we must drink with him the cup of suffering. As Christopher William Jones put it: 'From Cana to Palm Sunday, to his arrest in the garden, the kiss of Judas, the denial of Peter, to his condemnation by the masses, to the cross, there is his example. And his example is a condemnation for men of every century who think that Christianity can be easily lived, who think that to be a human being is an easy thing.'[9] For this reason, Barnabas Ahern sees 'fellowship in Christ's sufferings' as the inevitable result of the 'tension and struggle between life in Christ and life in the flesh'.[10]

Michel Quoist points out that this is a consequence of the command to love: 'I opened the door to one person and all of a sudden there are people coming in . . . hundreds, thousands. I can't close the door.' It's surely a picture reminiscent of Jesus so pressed by the crowds that he had to talk from the boat, that the paralytic had to be lowered down to him through the roof tiles, that he escaped across the lake only for the crowds to catch up with him and in all these situations 'his heart going out to them because they were like sheep without a shepherd'. For each of those who come—Quoist continues—we must be prepared to look at them and say 'I'm with you no matter what you do, no matter what you are, no matter where you are, no matter where you go, and I will help you all that I can. God grant that it crushes me instead of you.'[11]

Raymond Brown says that for the minister or priest who tries to follow Christ's ministry suffering must be the sign of the truth of apostolic service. He must be a man who bears Jesus' death pangs in his own body (2 Cor. 4:10), a man who finds no rest but is afflicted at every turn, from struggles without and anxieties within (2 Cor. 7:5). Paul was clear what Christ's pattern of life demanded. We see the anguish of a man who feels himself both unappreciated and humanly inadequate, yet through his very weakness all the more valuable a servant of Jesus Christ. We see how he relied on Our Lord's pledge: 'My grace is enough for you: my power is at its best in weakness.' (2 Cor. 12:9) This again mirrors the suffering servant's reliance in his tribulations on the pledge of God.[12]

Karl Rahner emphasises that such faith and trust in a minister or priest who follows Christ 'is the faith of a man of prayer—mystical contemplation—or it is nothing'. The steadfastness of our servant in the last canticle was only made possible by the closeness of God, because of the disciple's ear. Our Lord was the man of nights of prayer on the mountain, the man of the garden of Gethsemane. The prayer spoken of—Karl Rahner went on—cannot mean the private luxury of cultivating a beautiful soul. The prayer must be wrung from the cruelty of life by the deeds and anguish of faith. The preacher in turn would do well to remember that to speak of the luxury of a beautiful soul comes across as sickly and irrelevant, especially to the young who are more honest in their reactions; he would come across better if he tried to speak of the very real sort of prayer Christ himself had to pray.

Rahner reminds us also that 'if our theology is not a theology on its knees', if it degenerates into an intellectual exercise concerned only with problems rather than a soul-searching quest for solutions, then that theology would no longer be worthy of the name, it would be mere nineteenth-century pomposity. We must, he says, prayerfully endure the darkness of life, even if our prayer means sharing Jesus' bloody sweat in Gethsemane, his abandonment by God on the cross. In these days, when modern theologians get accused so often of betraying the Church by speculations which are regarded as at least useless if not positively damaging to the foundations of the Church, this comes as a reminder that their role too is that of the suffering servant with the only answers to be found on their knees amid the harsh reality of life.

In this light, Karl Rahner describes the priest who would follow Christ in the modern world as the 'man with the pierced heart'—and in describing the priest he outlines for me the fundamental characteristics of what is needed from the Christian counsellor:

> His office will not carry weight through social prestige, but only through the attractive vigour of his own personal experience of God, a man whose life is visibly invested not in a carefully delineated role as ecclesiastical civil servant but in a vocation where he is totally committed to listen to all, where every individual matters, where there are no painkillers for the dreadful disappointment of existence such as the pursuit of money, position or even the enjoyment of his hobbies— where the power of grace is not measured triumphally in numbers or success but accepted as present not only within one's endeavours but also outside. Such a man who has the courage to experience grace and to know desolation of heart, to be faithful, to follow conscience for no reward, to love the man furthest away as neighbour . . . discovers his wretched heart . . . and his heart is pierced. He will then look on the one whom they have pierced and feel the wounds which that pierced man has driven into his inmost being. Then perhaps he will keep starting up out of the sleeping round of the ecclesiastical functionary. Fear of betraying his true mission and grace will pierce his heart. He will flee from himself to him who alone is our hope and future. He will pray: Lord, by your heart make me through your omnipotent grace the man with the pierced heart who alone can be your priest or minister.[13]

Such Christian ministers or counsellors—if they are to follow Christ—should not be afraid to share that anguish and uncertainty with those to whom they are privileged to minister, for they are surrounded with the same uncertainty. It is a false virtue to be a twentieth-century Stoic and it has often and in many ways rendered the modern Christian irrelevant in the face of a generation which refuses to take things at face value and searches deeper into the heart and motives. It can completely nullify our witness to and following of Christ, the incarnate love of God, the Suffering Servant. Instead, we must face our shortcomings ourselves and then face the world with an honesty that makes no pretence of 'plaster-imaged piety' but confronts it with a naked desire to serve, a desire that exposes us to pain and hurt.

127

Only a few suffering servants would be needed to shatter once and for all the smug, rather comfortable middle-class or upper working-class image which encases the Christian Church and is so removed from the Galilean who stood on the fringes of Jewish society challenging its values ... and ours today.

Clearly, this expression of the meaning of Christ's life in terms of the Songs of the Servant of Yahweh is only one strand of New Testament thought, though it is a more important one than has often been realised. It must be balanced by the understanding of Jesus as a prophet. Here, however, we have to make qualifications because the early Church deliberately avoided calling him a prophet because they saw him as so much more than a prophet. Similarly, we have to balance the presentation of Christ as the Suffering Servant with what Joachim Jeremias highlights as crucial in the early Christian proclamation of his message. In him we find the 'return of the quenched spirit'. Here we have an idea with a long history. At the time of the Patriarchs, it was believed that all pious and upright men had the spirit of God. When Israel in a later age committed sin with the golden calf, God was seen as limiting the spirit to chosen men, prophets, high priests and kings. With the deaths of the last writing prophets, Haggai, Zechariah and Malachi, the spirit was seen as being quenched because of the sin of Israel. Still later, God was believed to speak only through the 'echo of his voice'. God was understood as silent. People longed for the spirit to come, to return with his message of hope.

It is against this background then that Jesus proclaimed that the time of the spirit had already begun with the preaching of John the Baptist. The New Testament was next to understand and speak about Jesus as God's last and final messenger. He is the 'return of the quenched spirit': as such he speaks with authority in word and deed. The combination of Christ speaking with authority and Christ suffering with and for the helpless, means the dawn of salvation.

The Gospels
When we turn to the gospels, we find four quite different but clearly sculptured presentations of who they believed the early Christ to be. They were written a long time after the first proclamation of the Good News of Christ risen from the dead

128

(the bare bones of the Christian message in the first sermons, the kerygma). The further spoken development of Christ's message by the apostles (the Didache) had also played its part long since. So had the written collections of sayings and doings of Jesus—and so presumably had the Aramaic Q version of the gospel which is postulated as preceding Mark's. The ground had been prepared for the four theological presentations we know as the gospels of Matthew, Mark, Luke and John. What is striking is that despite this variegated pre-history, these four theological presentations have elements in them which justify seeing Christ as having an approach to people which has many undoubted parallels with what we would describe today as the non-judgmental counselling approach. The shorthand speaks of the 'counselling of Jesus' but that is an anachronism: nonetheless it is a shorthand that has more justification than would appear at first sight.

Mark's attempt, about 60 AD, to write a Greek gospel was a failure in technical terms (no order or consistent tenses or structured writing), but a striking success as a vivid unspoilt picture of the personality of Jesus as the Son of God in our full reflected sense of that phrase. Scene follows scene, almost haphazardly stirring in both by-standers and readers alike doubt, wonder, anger, fear, surprise, delight, relief and gradual realisation that this man was prophet, Messiah and Son of God. The original ending (16:8) presents an open-ended challenge which is typical of what Christ is presented as evoking. He doesn't teach neat statements or set out black and white packages of rules—or give easy answers. He leaves us to question ourselves—and to search for answers. The two Marys and Salome 'came out and ran away from the tomb because they were frightened out of their wits; and they said nothing to a soul, for they were afraid. . . .' (Mk. 16:8) This fear of course has a particular meaning developed throughout the gospel. It is not a negative cringing but rather a sense of awe and reverence that makes us pause and wonder. It is illuminating that the early Church used two other endings to reinforce the unspoken positive side of their faith that in their fears and wonderings the 'Lord worked with them and proved that their preaching was true by the miracles that were performed' and 'Jesus himself sent out through his disciples, from the east to the west, the sacred and ever-living message of eternal salvation.' (Mk. 16:19 and Mk. 16:10)

129

Matthew's faultless Greek writing also fails to be a piece of Greek literature but employs the much loved Jewish parallelism to open out thought patterns rather than neat presentations. In five great discourses, with an Infancy section at the beginning and a Passion narrative at the end, the old law and the kingdom are presented as being fulfilled in the new law and the kingdom. Jesus as the Messiah and as divine is presented majestically and with dignity as the fount of contemplation. It reflects the pattern of the Christian liturgy with its invitation to listen to the narrative, take part in the discourse and only then come to encounter the Christ who is unfolded.

Luke's beautiful Greek presentation is of Christ as the universal saviour (all Adam's descendants) whose message is for 'all flesh': a saviour who is descended from and preaches to the outlawed poor, the *anawim*, the ones on the fringes of society, the bruised reeds of Isaiah. He breaks down national and religious barriers such as those with Samaria. Once again there is the awe, balanced here with a clear message of joy. As we continue in this chapter to explore the counselling of Jesus, we will see how St Luke gives us an unforgettable portrait of Christ's caring and sensitivity to the disadvantaged.

John's reputation for high theology has been balanced in recent years by the developed understanding of the rich Jewish character of the events he used to illustrate his message (these were once seen as mutually exclusive characteristics). He emphasises that the Word became flesh and is the interpenetration of the divine with the human. Here the focus is Christ's weakness, suffering and even humour; and paradoxically, the concept 'Christ the counsellor' survives the longer process of handing on of the sources before the gospel was written. This too we will return to as we explore the Christ who emerges: he is seen counselling Nicodemus, the woman at the well, the woman caught in adultery and the like.

The Parables

Great controversy used to be caused by Jesus' use of the parable. People got confused when he told them, 'The secret of the Kingdom of God is given to you, but to those who are outside everything comes in parables, so that they may see and see again, but not perceive; may hear and hear again, but not understand; otherwise they might be converted and be forgiven.' (Mk. 4:10–11) This is only a sad summation of Jesus' failure with those who shut their minds to what he was saying, and not a description of what he intended by using the parables. The purpose of the parables is quite different. It was to explain and to teach in an open-ended way: the crowds took so much out of them and the disciples were encouraged to explore with Our Lord the further meaning that can be developed out of them (Mt. 13:36; Jn. 16:29). His picture of the kingdom which is taught through the parables was so different from what was expected that it is hardly surprising that even the disciples had to have them explained time and time again.[14]

The parable strictly speaking is based on simile but the metaphors used in allegories have a place (though nothing like the exaggerated versions in the Fathers). Our Lord's use of the parable is mainly of similes opened into stories and this allows the person listening to respond to the material from where they are. This was helped by the fact that Jesus used illustrations from everyday life in a rural Galilean setting: outdoor scenes of hill country farming and shepherding mixed up with domestic scenes in a simple one-room house (Lk. 11:5–8). The homes of the rich are seen only through the kitchen door.

The parables often follow the 'rule of three' for good stories or jokes: such as is illustrated by the standard formula jokes about 'the Englishman, the Scot and the Irishman'. Very often we have to keep reminding ourselves that many elements are there for the sake of the story. There are problems too of bits being added on to stories in the course of the history of the development of the New Testament. Yet once we cut through the minor irritations of the bits we don't understand, the parables shine out as central to Christ's approach to people. He gives a challenging and novel message—and often leaves his listeners scratching their heads in puzzlement or, if they are antagonistic, hopping mad in anger. C.H. Dodd[15] and Joachim Jeremias[16] suggest very strongly that many of the parables, rather than being nice stories with a moral are part of Jesus' vigorous assault on established values by his preaching of the kingdom of God. Be that as it may, they are certainly designed to enable the listener to ask fundamental questions about themselves and to journey in searching and prayer for new answers. That is precisely what the counsellor tries to do.

In *Disturbing the Peace*, Eamonn Bredin gives a brilliant exposition of the story of the Good Samaritan. He makes it plain that Jesus doesn't put into words any conclusion he wanted people to draw from the story. Instead, he leaves the challenge to the Jewish audience: they are compelled to answer the question 'Who was neighbour . . . ?' with the answer 'The Samaritan was the neighbour.' And then he goes on to voice the inner feelings of the Jew:

> I am being forced/freed to say what cannot be said. I am to put words on what sticks in my throat, to voice what chokes me, to join two words never before found united in the entire history of separation between Judea and Samaria—the words Samaritan and neighbour. This conclusion is revolting and sickening. It demands that my world view, my familiar horizons, my understanding, my whole value system be called into question.

And so he continues to show how Jesus opened out the inner prejudices and presuppositions of the listener—not by telling them things but by enabling them to question their own attitudes for themselves. This enabling process is counselling. Fr Bredin goes on:

> Parables alert us to what it might mean to define the world in a radically new way. In his parables Jesus tries to draw his hearers out of their closed, self-centred world toward the new world whose moving centre is the kingdom of God. His parables start within the world they recognise but, though the power of metaphor, he then confronts them with the paradox: This is not our world after all! The shattering of the everyday world brings them to the threshold at the same time. The parables dislocate and disturb, as they seek to draw the hearers away from the old and toward the new. A challenging alternative is presented. Only the hearers can decide which world they will choose.[17]

In parallel with this, of course, choice is at the very essence of what the counsellor leaves with the person cared for.

The Miracles of Jesus

First instinct might lead us to feel that the miracles of Jesus have little relation to seeing him as a counsellor—even though every counsellor hopes at times for miracles! Modern studies, however, have moved the emphasis from defining miracles negatively as violations of nature to seeing them as positive signs—perceived only by those capable of 'wondering'—of the fact that all reality is included in the historical dispensation of God, that God is working behind the extraordinary signs with the same power that is active in ordinary ways at every point of our existence. The Greek word of wonder (*teras*) is never used on its own for the gospel miracles. Instead 'sign' (*semeion*) or 'work' (*ergon*) in St John and 'act of power' in the rest of the New Testament are words which emphasise the fact that the gospel miracles are used as vehicles of the gospel message, that they are lessons-in-action as it were. They are the meeting place of the message with the call to believe the message. St John distinguishes seeing the sign as a real pointer to something deeper from not seeing the significance at all; and then—at a deeper level—with those who have seen, he distinguishes responding by an act of faith (Jn. 2:11; 4:53; 11:15; 12:42 etc.) from refusing to believe (8:47). In other words, miracles don't miraculously convince people by a miraculous short-cut. At the end of the day, we can only be drawn to accept their message because of the authenticity of the religious testimony of the ones who saw themselves clearly as eye-witnesses of the miracles of Jesus.[18]

Three quotations illustrate for me the compatibility of Jesus' miracles with that aspect of his personality which we can identify as a counselling approach. The first is from Louis Morden:

> There is on the one hand a remarkable sobriety, austerity and simplicity which contrasts with the showmanship and fairground atmosphere on the other. The dignity, seriousness, the self-forgetfulness of Jesus, the atmosphere of prayer, contrast with the trances, the fantasies, the trickery and the greed of the wonder-workers. In the gospels, there is no miracle that is futile, trivial or unwholesome, such as abound in the marvels of mythology.[19]

He points out there are no punitive miracles, no thirst for the marvellous, no miracles in infancy or in the passion, none attributed to John the Baptist, and that there is an abundance of details of no real interest which have nonetheless a startlingly authentic ring. 'The narratives are perfectly consonant with the person of the Lord, with his message and his work of salvation, with the symbolism of the sacraments and the language of the parables.

The second is from the Dutch Catechism

A miracle, according to Scripture, is something in which man sees God at work . . . But the word is used above all for events in which God's saving power is very specially manifest. They occur in the New Testament in connection with Christ's goodness, striking events which arouse wonder and have a definite significance . . . miracles teach man that he does not know what can happen within himself and in the world— 'There are more things in heaven and earth, Horatio, than are dreamt of in your philosophy.'[20]

This continued after the Church was founded, both in the sacraments and in the Lord confirming the message by the signs that attended it. These signs—these miracles—continue in the Church today, at Lourdes and in the lives of the saints. As in Our Lord's time, they at least make us wonder and they open us just that little bit more to being able to see God who works among us in Christ.

The third is from Hans Küng:

Jesus would be misunderstood if he were regarded as a practitioner of healing and a specialist in miracles, burdening himself methodically with all man's frailties. His activity must not be misinterpreted in a scientific sense.

Jesus would likewise be misunderstood if he were regarded merely as a pastor and confessor, concerned only with man's soul and spirit. His activity must not be interpreted in a spiritistic sense.

Hence the message of God's kingdom is aimed at man in all his dimensions, not only at man's soul but at the *whole* man in his mental and material existence, in his whole concrete, suffering world. And it holds for *all* men: not only the strong, young, healthy, capable whom the world so likes to exalt, but also the weak, sick, old, incapable, whom the world so likes to forget, to overlook, to neglect. Jesus did not merely talk, but also intervened in the field of sickness and injustice.[21]

The way Christ intervenes in the world and our lives has to be taken into account. Eamonn Bredin is worth returning to in his book *Disturbing the Peace*. He speaks of the Gerasene demoniac, one of the living dead to whom Christ crosses over to treat as a human being and thus reintegrate and heal. He then broadens the issues:

Here we meet many of the themes that we find in the narratives or miracles and exorcisms. Jesus is at hand, ready to step in and save those who are not free. He will not be prevented by religious, social or legal considerations. Jesus is against all evil. He leads the fight to liberate others, confronting it head on. When he acts, those outside are drawn in—people pass from violence to calm, from hate to love, from being beside themselves to coming to themselves, from incomprehension to truth, from opposition to discipleship.

The miracle stories underline the power Jesus brought into the world, the power of the kingdom of God's love. Even as they do so, however, they open out an approach that always encourages both the person benefitting and those who see the exercise of power to think and respond for themselves as free human beings. Old values and dependencies are seen to be inadequate and a new readiness to respond to God's love and transforming power emerges from the meeting with God's gentle loving power. Eamonn Bredin makes another important point when he stresses that normally we won't have any dramatic miracles as signs to sort us out, but there are signs if we can but open ourselves to them:

Jesus and those who accept him are happy to allow God's future to emerge gently, hiddenly, and always in a surprising way. Thus, no sign is given, for God is not like that. Jesus wishes only to point to the true God, not to prove something about himself. Abba is the source of what is done through Jesus. He must not be used to draw attention to himself. He must always point beyond to Abba. Jesus proclaims that this God-given transformation is beginning to take place. What is happening may be slight and appear to be of little significance compared to the brute weight of human suffering that effects his contemporaries, but it is its significance, its symbolic value, that is important.[22]

If Christ does not impose by his authority but instead points gently to the God beyond, so surely should the Christian care-er, priest or minister.

135

The Theology of Christ

The modern theology of Christ, which tries to restore the balance in our understanding of him from an overemphasis on his divinity to an appreciation of his very real humanity, would seem to confirm the relevance and significance of regarding Christ as having an approach to people which can reasonably be described as a Christian non-judgmental counselling approach. Ladislaus Boros in *God is with us* provides a very useful starting point. The questions he considers are simple ones: how he exercised the profound human attitudes which we call love, humility and mercy; why he manifested no repentance; why his faith and his hopes were not, like those of other men, directed into the darkness; in what way he was silent; why he was a stranger in the sphere of human existence. In this way, to quote Boros, 'we shall perceive that he is so different—loved, spoke, showed humility and pity and so forth so differently—that his being goes beyond the bounds of what is purely human'. Only in this way, he maintains, can we overcome the sad reality that our knowledge of Jesus has become largely mechanical, lifeless and rigid. he concludes his book: 'In Jesus, God appears as kindness and charm. If we but touch the surface of the Gospels, the form of Christ will reveal itself to us and if we cultivate a loving intimacy with him, we shall find God himself.' That kindness and charm sound very like the qualities we imagine in 'Christ the Counsellor'.[23]

In *Jesus Christ* Yves Congar builds up from a picture of 'what Jesus learned of God revealing himself in poverty, of the prayer of Christ, of the preaching of Christ' to a final consideration of Jesus Christ as 'Lord of the Church and indeed of the world'.[24] This is surely the right balance, not losing sight of what is finally appreciated but not missing out on the development to the understanding of that reality. The French biblical scholar F.X. Durwell looks at Christ from a relatively straightforward but helpful point of view.

Jesus was God's son but there were within him quite considerable elements which God's glorifying holiness did not enter: not only his body but also his faculties which brought him into contact with us were not so completely possessed by the life of the Spirit that Christ could not suffer fear and anguish, that the son of the immortal God could not succumb to death.[25]

Edward Schillebeeckx goes a step further. 'To be a man is a process of becoming a man: Jesus' manhood grew throughout his earthly life, finding its completion in the supreme moment of the incarnation, his death, resurrection and exaltation.'[26] The significance of that phrase for counselling is clear. It calls to mind at once the standard book by Eugene Kennedy, *On becoming a Counsellor*, where he details the whole process of growth within oneself that is the only basis for being able to offer support to the same process in others at the critical or stressful points of their lives.[27] It finds an immediate echo too in the Letter to the Hebrews where the writer gives the unforgettable portrait of Christ in terms of being the one mediator between God and man, the High Priest who has effected the link and has done so because he has known and lived through and developed through all the weakness of our human condition except sin.

That experience of human weakness is the foundation of all counselling. Eamonn Bredin brings all his experience in Ireland and Peru to describe the compassion (*rahimin*) or tender, vulnerable love that builds the necessary bridges of pastoral care:

The gospels tell us that Jesus is moved with pity for a leper (Mk. 1:41) that he saw a great throng and he had compassion on them (Mk. 6:34), and 'I have compassion on the crowd because they have nothing to eat' (Mk. 8:2). He enters into the fears and the pain, the tears and the worries and the anxieties of people in order to transform them. 'Do not fear, only believe' (Mk. 5:36); 'Why do you make a tumult and weep?' (Mk. 5:39); 'Take heart, it is I, have no fear' (Mk. 6:50). The phrase 'Do not be anxious' recurs. He responds to infirmity and sickness in the same way: 'He had compassion on them and healed their sick' (Mt. 14:14). When he meets the widow of Naim on her way to bury her son he is moved and enters into her grief, and he had compassion on her and said to her 'Do not weep,' (Lk. 7:13). Again, in the context of grief at another death we are told: When Jesus saw her weeping, and the Jews who came with her also weeping, he was deeply moved in spirit and troubled (these are equivalent to the root meaning of what we translate as compassion). . . and Jesus wept.

So the Jews said, 'See how he loved him' (Jn. 11:33–37). In his stories, the Samaritan had compassion (Lk. 10:33), the king has compassion but the unmerciful servant has none (Mt. 18:23–35). Similarly, Jesus is moved to compassion and reaches out to and touches the untouchables. He touches the lepers and the beggars and the blind, he grasps the hands of the palsied and the crippled and the insane. He draws all into himself because he is compassionate as his Father is compassionate.[28]

The next stage is taking that caring to 'the poor and the sinners' and this of course is the area into which Christian counselling in our modern world must also penetrate.

The compelling edge of Christ's compassion is seen too from a full appreciation in theology of his humanity and the exploring of Christ's growth in knowledge and consciousness. This is at the outward circle of the concentric meditations on his divinity and humanity which must mark both theology and spirituality, but the good sense of it is illustrated very well by the squirmings and evasions we find in earlier theologians such as St Thomas Aquinas and Cajetan in trying to explain texts such as Mark 13:32 where Jesus says of the Last Day: 'But as for that day or hour, nobody knows it, neither the angels of heaven, nor the son; no one but the Father.' In fact, such texts do imply that in his human consciousness Our Lord was not aware of such things, he just did not know. As St Luke put it he 'increased in wisdom, in stature, and in favour with God and man.'

This process continued throughout his life and would only reach completion once he had passed through death and achieved in full human consciousness that beatific vision which can only penetrate a human nature fully when the chains of weak and otherwise normally sinful flesh have been released. As Yves Congar says:

All the filial obedience of Christ is summed up in his passion. . . . He had practiced it throughout his life and, by this very practice, he had humanly better understood and deepened it. The human feelings, the dispositions of heart and of will, by means of which Jesus effected our salvation had gradually been formed in his experience as a young Jew and in his education at Nazareth by Mary and Joseph.[29]

138

Karl Adam in *The Christ of Faith* emphasises the letter to the Hebrews as it speaks of Jesus learning obedience through the things he suffered and goes on to speak of Jesus 'learning the details of his passion only by way of his advancing personal experience in immediate contact with his situation, which daily became more critical'.[30] Piet Schoonenberg speaks of Jesus' 'choice of career' in leaving joinery to start preaching and how he 'only gradually became clear about the circumstances of his life and the direction his life should take. His horizon broadens out from the lost sheep of Israel to Jew and Gentile, and his mission develops from that of a prophet to one proclaiming salvation for all.'[31]

St Luke's Gospel has Jesus coming to a turning point, a life decision, when he set his feet resolutely on Jerusalem, realising only then that he had to face rejection or death. E. Gutwenger speaks of the same sort of 'development in his understanding of his mission'.[32] Von Balthasar points out that 'Christ's perfection essentially consists of an obedience which does not anticipate, of a patience that is the model of ours'.[33] Brother Gabriel Moran points out that 'whereas medieval theology made no distinction between an immediate knowledge of God and the beatific vision, contemporary theology attributes to Christ a direct link with God that is not necessarily beatifying when he is on earth.'[34]

Karl Rahner expands the question best of all and time after time he speaks of a spiritual and religious development in Jesus. 'There was in him as in us a history of his own personal self-interpretation of himself to himself'. He points out that beatific vision, as we understand it, was impossible to Christ hanging in agony and abandonment on the cross: 'this was not the consciousness of one who questions, doubts, learns, is surprised, is deeply moved, is tempted, is overwhelmed by a deadly feeling of being forsaken by God'.[35] There were things he did not know and things he only gradually learnt—and it is that reality which makes the thesis of Christ the counsellor tenable. As Fr Louis Evely insists 'The Christ of the gospels was weary and relaxed in turn, worried and unsure or in turn confident, encouraged and disillusioned, full of zeal and tempted to despair.'[36] Such a man prayed because he needed to pray amid the stresses of human living: in those same stresses the Christian care-er or counsellor will have to pray first and then teach in carrying on his message. It's a question of balance.

139

Fran Ferder sums up the human feelings which Christ showed. One passage encapsulates the issue and its implications for Christian communication, caring and indeed counselling:

Jesus experienced the full range of human emotion:
He felt sorry (Lk. 7:13)
Moved with pity, Jesus stretched out his hand (Mk. 1:41)
How often I have longed (Lk. 13:34)
And sadness came over him (Mt. 26:37)
Then, grieved . . . he looked angrily around (Mk. 3:5)
He . . . summoned those he wanted (Mk. 3:13)
He was indignant (Mk. 10:21)
Filled with joy (Lk. 10:21)
He shed tears (Lk. 19:41–42)
I have longed (Lk. 22:15)
I have loved you (Jn. 15:9)
He was astonished (Mt. 8:10)

Jesus was filled with an almost inexpressible zeal to accomplish his mission: I have come to bring fire to the earth, and how I wish it were blazing already! (Lk. 12:49). One can feel the yearning in those words, the ache moving through every muscle of his body. Jesus knew the pain and disappointment of rejection, the agony of sadness. He experienced the kind of intense longing that pulls at the heart and gnaws in the stomach. At times it moved him to tears, wet and salty expressions of feeling. He churned with anger, struggled with impatience, and cherished times of joy and excitement. His pulse quickened with compassion, and his face mellowed in tenderness. He knew love.[37]

This sister from the United States goes on to expound the importance of seeing Christ in this way and the reason why I include here so many snippets from modern theology. 'The attempt to over-spiritualize the emotional life leads eventually to deeply buried grief, resentments, angers, sexual desires, fears, attractions and a full range of locked-in feeling experiences. Sometimes offering up an uncomfortable feeling is not prayer at all, but a religious name for psychological repression.' In her book she looks squarely at how anger was a part of Christ's spiritual life and must be part of ours.

140

Particularly helpful is her parallel with the model of development outlined by Maslow where his research shows that all of us as human beings—and of course Jesus in his human development also—have essentially the same basic needs and each of us will be a healthier human being if we can manage to have our needs met in an ascending hierarchy of development. At the bottom are physiological needs: food, water, shelter, sex, whatever is needed for survival. When these are met we can move on to our safety needs: security, stability, freedom from fear. Only then do we move on to face acceptance needs: having love, friends, intimacy, feeling a part of other people's lives. Then we seek to meet our esteem needs: feeling important, useful, competent, needed. The self-actualising needs of being able to reach one's potential, developing one's gifts and becoming an integrated human being stem from this whole process.

This was at first as far as Maslow and his associates would go, but the interesting part for the theology of Christian development is that another level of development proved to be demanded by human behaviour. This is the stage of self-transcendence—genuine holiness—where we become able to move beyond our own needs, often in dramatic ways, to serve the needs of others. It can obviously be argued how much our needs along the way have to be met before we can achieve self-transcendence. The atheist or agnostic will maintain that the whole process has to be worked through if one is to become a healthy human being and that this is open to us as human beings. Still to be explored is the Christian response in terms of our need of God's grace in Christ to be able to travel that road—and particularly to travel it when some of the earlier stages of fulfillment of human need are made impossible for us.

Rather than eliminating the scope for the fundamental doctrine of grace, this analysis may well give a clear setting for our dependence on the grace of the Holy Spirit at every stage of our journey: a firm foundation for seeing the Spirit working in every human being (because God wants all to be saved and because Christ laid down his life for all), and a pattern for understanding a little better the transforming power of Christ's divinity in his humanity (the hypostatic union). It may also make clear the theological foundation for the opening out which is counselling to be in fact the pastoral approach which most respects the mystery of the Spirit in that process of development in every human being of whatever culture or religion or attitude to life.

Christ's Listening

Both Fran Ferder in *Words made Flesh* and Duncan Buchanan in *The Counselling of Jesus*[38] highlight this characteristic of Jesus' life and mission. It is central to what he does and how he approaches it. Before we turn to their more specific treatment of Christ's listening, however, it might be as well to establish quite categorically the context within which it takes place. In *The Church with a Human Face*, Edward Schillebeeckx outlines what we know of Christ's mission:

> To a great degree Jesus' action consisted in establishing social community, opening up communication, above all where 'excommunication' and rejection were officially in force: in respect of public sinners, publicans making themselves rich from the poor, lepers, and others, whoever and whatever were 'unclean'. These are the ones he seeks out, the ones with whom he eats. Jesus also singles out women, though they do not belong, like the men, to his group (although a later phase on the New Testament to some degree removes the distinctive character of Jesus' attitude to women). In all this Jesus is aware that he is acting as God would do. He translates God's action to human beings. His parables speak of the one lost sheep, a lost coin, a lost son. By his actions Jesus wants to make clear to his fellow believers, who are irritated at his dealings with the unclean, that God turns towards lost and vulnerable people. Jesus acts as God acts. So with him there is a claim that in his actions and words God himself is present.[39]

On this basis, Christ himself proceeds to free people from need and distress and then sends his disciples out with the task of healing people and making them whole.

When we ask about the 'how' of Christ's coming, the Jesuit Gerard W. Hughes in *God of Surprises* is extremely helpful:

> Because he was at one with his Father, therefore Christ is no respecter of persons and does not need the support of rank or status. His own description of himself as 'the Son of Man' is,

according to some commentators, the translation of Aramaic slang for 'an ordinary bloke' or in Scottish terminology 'an ordinary punter'. His being, as man, is the reflection of God's own being and therefore, although in himself he is best described as being 'for the Father', to us he appears as 'the man for others', for it is the nature of God to be for us.

This we see summed up in John's account of the Last Supper. 'This is the action of God translated into human terms, the God who washes feet.' On this foundation, Fr Hughes goes on to speak of Christ's 'poverty of spirit' and the 'poverty of spirit' asked of us as Christians:

> Spiritual poverty is a phrase which describes one aspect of Christ's relationship with the Father, namely that he was so anchored and rooted in the life of his Father that nothing could possess him, neither his desire to have ('Turn these stones into bread'), nor his desire to count and be important ('leap down from the pinnacle of the Temple'), nor the desire to have power ('Take over the kingdoms of the world'). St Paul expresses his own poverty of spirit in these words to the Philippians: 'I know how to be poor and I know how to be rich too. I have been through my initiation and now I am ready for anything anywhere: full stomach or empty stomach, poverty or plenty. There is nothing I cannot master with the help of the One who gives me strength.' (4:12–13)[40]

Another Jesuit, Peter G. van Breeman, exemplifies what Hughes is saying from a quite different angle. He uses the word *prautes*, a characteristic of the Jesus of the Gospels and his essential attitude to life; and in this he links with Ladislaus Boros, *God is with us*, which we mentioned earlier.[41] It is translated as meekness, gentleness or mildness—or peacefulness, humility, unobtrusiveness, modesty, lowliness, calmness or recollection. He suggests that 'with a still heart' may be the best attempt and this clearly opens the door to considerations of the quality needed for listening or for counselling. He doesn't make the application, but what he says leads naturally to this conclusion. *Prautes* describes the person who radiates a still heart: when St Paul says that we should 'clothe ourselves with Christ' it is *prautes* which sums that up. It is the spirituality outlined in the eight beatitudes and reflected in the fruits of the Spirit in Galatians 5:22 (love, joy, peace, patience, kindness, goodness, trustfulness, gentleness and self-control). Matthew's account of Palm Sunday (21:5) describes the man of *prautes* as opposed to the triumphal entry of the Roman general after victory. The stillness is internal, the 'peace of knowing oneself accepted by God as one is and abandoning oneself to his love. It is to rest secure with God in genuine closeness to him, surrendering to him without struggle or strain.'[42]

Fr van Breeman likens it to what Muslims say when they observe that 'two people have only learned to love one another when they can be silently together'. Ladislaus Boros again: 'Jesus came from silence. This was his home and he had to struggle to achieve speech. Man came out of turmoil and noise, and silence is a task for him.' It brings 'thoughtfulness and wisdom, sensitiveness and sympathy to our words'. This makes it the foundation for listening and counselling. It takes courage and strength of steel: 'The early Christians realized the power of meekness, the sacred character and strength of defencelessness. A new force entered the world with the martyr who trembled, but stood firm, not revolting against anyone, and not debasing his suffering by ill will or vanity. It is a great good fortune to meet a truly gentle person: it can mark a whole life.' 1 Peter 3:15–16 takes the attitude into conversations: 'Simply reverence the Lord Christ in your hearts, and always have your answer ready for people who ask you the reason for the hope that you all have. But give it with courtesy and respect and with a clear conscience.' And James 3:13, 17: 'If there are any wise and learned men among you, let them show it by their good lives, with humility and wisdom in their actions. . . . The wisdom that comes down from above is essentially something pure; . . . it is full of compassion and shows itself by doing good.'

Duncan Buchanan emphasises Jesus' qualities of listening by looking at two incidents where insights into his listening are secondary to the main thrust of the story. The first is blind Bartimaeus in Mk 10:46–52. The dramatic build-up to Christ's entry to Jerusalem is interrupted. 'Jesus stopped', neither too busy nor too popular to stop and listen. He makes the beggar come to him, presupposing nothing even though he can see that the man is blind. Buchanan notes 'This is taking the other person seriously and allowing him the freedom both to know and state his problem in his own way and with his own insights.'[43]

The second incident is the woman with the flow of blood in Mk 5:25–34. Again the scene is busy, with the healing of the man with the legion of demons and the call from Jairus for Jesus to come and heal his daughter. The desperate woman takes the risk of touching his garments. This is the risk of faith to which Jesus responds. He then stops: 'turned about and with the crowd jostling him, he was still able to perceive the real need and act of faith in a sea of want'. Now that's a bit poetic but the point is clear nonetheless. From these two incidents, Buchanan—who lectures on counselling in South Africa—goes on to illustrate how hearing is a central theme in John's gospel. In Chapters 5 and 8, he has major discourses about the various levels of listening that are the development of faith in Jesus' listeners. Peter's response in chapter 6 is the core of what is asked of Christ's followers: 'Lord, who shall we go to? You have the message of eternal life, and we believe; we know that you are the Holy One of God.' (Jn. 6:68–69). Central to our purpose here, however, is Jesus' listening and two examples given by Buchanan are the conversations with Nicodemus and with the Samaritan woman which would indeed repay a lot of study for anyone interested in Christian counselling or pastoral care.

The Samaritan woman (Jn. 4:1–42) came at another stopping point. Jesus breaks every convention and talks to the much des-pised Samaritan woman. He 'not only listens to her words, but perceives that behind her somewhat brash attitude lies a deep inadequacy and inability to relate, so that already she has had more husbands than she needs. The last husband cannot there-fore even be described as a husband.' The concentric circles of real listening are of course abundantly clear in the whole gentle unfolding of the situation and the changes that are visibly taking place in emotion and in attitude.

With Nicodemus (Jn. 3:1–21):

The interview starts with Nicodemus making compliments, but that is not where Jesus is, or what he needs. Nicodemus is faced with a truth which he cannot understand, and every time he takes it literally Jesus hears not only the incom-prehension but also the defensiveness. It's almost as though Nicodemus does not want to hear things beyond his compre-hension or outside his traditional ways of looking at things.

145

Yet Jesus hears the fear, hears the fascination too and pushes through to a different set of conclusions than those represented by Nicodemus.

The conversation could be analysed quite differently but the general point is inescapable, namely that by listening, Jesus freed Nicodemus to face other challenges and ultimately to have him as a defender when he was being tried for his life. While all the time we have to remember that these conversations are literary products rather than verbatim tape recordings, the basic perception of Jesus' approach seems to shine through; and all the modern studies of St John's gospel, which have reinstated the extent of his authentic reflection of the historical Palestinian happenings, combine to suggest very powerfully that the vivid picture of Christ the counsellor is an accurate one.

Fran Ferder situates her analysis of Jesus' listening in the general biblical idea of listening or contemplating as both God's response to creation (God rested on the seventh day) and the response asked of us. This seems to me to be overdrawn, but it may have a place. Be that as it may, Jesus is then highlighted as having been completely attuned to God's voice in creation (witness all his references to the beauty of nature). Lk. 2:46 presents him listening to the doctors in the Temple and asking them questions. This is theology rather than history but is still significant for Luke's attitude to Jesus. The temptations summary in all three synoptic gospels portray a man listening and engaging in a lonely struggle against the false attractions of life. It concludes: 'Man does not live on bread alone but on every word that comes from the mouth of God.' (Mt.4:4). Listening to God becomes listening to people. Ferder cites Jesus' listening to the seventy two disciples coming back to ask Jesus where he lived and the immediate invitation 'Come and see'. This Fran Ferder develops:

> One by one they come to him—the blind and the lame, the lepers and the paralytics, destitute people and people who commanded armies. There were Jewish leaders, civil leaders, tax collectors and prostitutes. There were honest seekers and curious bystanders. There were friends and there were enemies. They all came with their needs and their stories to this man whose very presence commanded attention. He listened to all

146

of them. He listened with such intensity that he heard much more than their words. In some he heard their faith as well as their pain. He listened and sent them away, not only physically healed, but with a new sense of inner peace.[44]

This whole process brought sadness, surprise, happiness, weariness, insight and self-discovery. In turn Jesus asked his audience to listen in such a way as to search for understanding. He quoted Isaiah: 'You will listen and listen again, but not understand. . . . For the heart of this nation has grown coarse, their ears are dull of hearing . . . for fear they should . . . hear with their ears, understand with their heart, and be converted and be healed by me.' (Mt. 13:15)

One last incident—the woman caught in adultery and threatened with being stoned to death—highlights dramatically not just Christ's listening to the outcast and to his own enemies, confronting the outcast and challenging him with her, but also emphasises that sort of non-judgmental counselling which opens the way to encouragement to an improved way of life. It is a theological presentation, an incident used to teach important lessons to the early Christian community; but it is also a story of caring and of gently confrontational listening. So many aspects of the incident go against the Jewish customs of the time and yet remain rooted in them that we are almost forced to conclude that it reflects an accurate picture of Christ as he was remembered and spoken about.

I hope that this short review of the modern theology of Christ will have disclosed that the concept of Christ the counsellor is not so much of a reading back into history as it might have seemed at first sight. To consider him in this way does in fact seem to unfold new and yet familiarly loved aspects of his compellingly attractive personality to the world of today. It also provides the theological foundation for seeing counselling as a Christian challenge.

Christ the Word of God

We have looked at Christ the Counsellor. We must now situate this concept in the whole context of modern theology if we are to see how the counselling approach was necessary for Christ's purpose and is even more necessary for the sort of culture we live in. As Denis Nineham points out:

If there is to be divine communication to men who live in history, it will inevitably be historically conditioned. If it is to be intelligible to those to whom it is made, it will have to be in terms of their institutions, assumptions and myths, which means that it will have to be in culturally conditioned terms. There is no possibility of a revelation which transcends culturally conditioned terms altogether and is given in terms which are not peculiar to any one culture but apply equally to all cultures.[45]

In other words: 'In the beginning was the Word and the Word was with God and the Word was God . . . and the Word became flesh.' John Calvin has his own way of putting it: 'God bends and lowering himself, lisps that we might hear and understand.' More recently Robert Webber, in *God Still Speaks*, makes an observation: 'True communication takes us through from the Incarnation to the whole theologies of grace and man's transformation.'[46] Protestant and Catholic theology come together in Barth and Küng to clarify that theology of grace. Then from one perspective after another, modern theologians build up the picture of Christ learning to communicate by listening to those around him and listening to God his Father in prayer. He is placed in a cosmological perspective by Hulsbosch, de Chardin, Schoonenberg and North; in an anthropological perspective by Rahner and Lowe; in a historical perspective by Pannenberg, Cullman and Moltmann; in a political perspective by liberation theology with J. B. Metz in Europe and Gutierrez, Segundo and Miranda in Latin America; and in a biblical perspective by Schillebeeckx, Vawter, Boros and countless others.

After the Second Vatican Council, the Catechetical Directory laid down for the Roman Catholic Church that the task of Christian education is 'so to present the humanity of Christ as to gradually open out an awareness of his humanity'.[47] To see his counselling as part of that process is yet another stage in becoming aware of his rounded humanity. As outlined already in this chapter, Christ worked within the categories of his historical situation to establish a real dialogue with people which enabled them to open out from their own rigid insecurities to face the questions raised not just by his message but more importantly by his whole person.

When we turn to the modern situation in which the Church has to carry on his work, things have changed dramatically with the communications revolution. In *God in a Box* Colin Morris suggests—and I believe rightly—that modern means of communication present alternative thinking beyond man's previous comprehension and so have changed the milieu of faith.[48] He begins with Edmond Carpentier's definition of a closed society as one in which there is a tight correlation between information and behaviour. In it the individual has no information to rely on and act on. Colin Morris believes we now live in the ultimate open society where we are presented with plenty of information for alternative patterns of behaviour but protect our sanity by blocking out a great deal of both the natural messages and the engineered messages which began the confusion. The result is what Bertrand Russell would call the development in ordinary people of 'the technique of suspended judgment' as a coping mechanism. This would be similar to what Sir John Eccles defines as 'inhibition', viz. the brain's ability to shut off when too many messages come in too quickly to be coped with. All this in turn is seen to lead to phenomena such as floating voters and floating believers. Avery Dulles quotes William Kuhn:

> The entertainment milieu has transformed the way in which we believe and are capable of believing. An absolute kind of belief, as well as a belief in absolutes, becomes increasingly difficult as the entertainment milieu trains people to believe tentatively and with elasticity. . . . The very concept of faith— to believe in that which you cannot see and understand— comes with difficulty to a generation which has depended, as perhaps no generation before, on its senses. . . .[49]

Lastly Colin Morris quotes Gregor Goethals in his analysis of television as the modern icon, resplendent with spiritual power.

> The heroes and heroines in the sacred icons were portrayed as exceptional human beings, though morally frail: their image witnesses a faith in a divine, transcendent being. The icons of technology, by contrast, portray a gospel that can deliver people from ugliness, age, even death and destruction. Central to the new faith is the belief that human nature is not constant and that people like products can continually be changed, up-dated, improved and packaged.[50]

149

His challenge to the Church is to find new ways of communicating the great adventure of faith.

The new uncertainty generated in the 'global village' of modern means of communication, where radio, television and video make so much so easily tangible, increases for me the pressure for the Church to stop preaching from a distance at people's uncertainties and learn to be content to begin just by listening patiently to hear where people are and what they are saying and what they are worried about. Only then can the Church begin to speak.

Michael Paul Gallagher[51] has analysed the pattern of changing faith in Ireland (changes which have already taken place in Britain) and makes it clear that there are many factors other than the mass media in what is acknowledged as the changed situation for faith. His schema speaks for itself of three types of society—three situations for faith:

The Impact of Social Change: Three situations for faith

	A	B	C
KIND OF SOCIETY	Stable, rural	More affluent etc: transition to more secular values	Urban technological complex
POSITION OF CHURCH	Dominant central	Religion an increasingly separate sphere; one influence among others	A marginal institution
TYPE OF 'UNBELIEF' FOUND	Non-practice by marginal individuals	Sub-groups fall away (youth workers etc.)	Non-belief by masses (including non-practice)
PASTORAL RESPONSES	Bring individuals back to the sacraments	Renew parish & church structures for better communication of Gospel	Critique of society; awaken basic question of God

Clearly my own response to that schema would be to suggest that the critique of society might well be counter-productive unless the listening to what is being said is our first response; and only after this that counselling has enabled a relationship to build, and find room naturally to share our faith insights on the basis of that sharing which is friendship.

Staying with theology, there is yet another area of renewed thinking which is even more fundamental as we explore the context in which counselling can be seen in Christian terms to be the properly respectful way to enter into a helping relationship and proper communication with other human beings. This is the theology of the Trinity. Robert Webber in *God Still Speaks* puts it this way:

> Since communication within the Godhead is personal and relational, we may conclude the same is true of all meaningful communication. The Father, the Son and the Holy Spirit do not communicate with each other as if each were outside or alienated from the other. The witness of true communication is that it is always expressed through love. Love is the basis of good relations, and therefore the context in which all good communication should take place. Certainly trinitarian communication stands in judgment on our attempts to communicate in our impersonal and non-relational ways. It sets up a standard for communication.[52]

This for me is important, not only for pointing to the face-to-face encounter at the heart of all communication but because the modern theology of the Trinity has made this more and not less relevant. Despite the criticism of Professor James Mackey[53], much of which has validity for refining the theory, Karl Rahner's work on the Trinity[54] may well provide a foundation. Instead of the old model of the Trinity which was based on God's reflection being so perfect as to result in the Word as a person equal in dignity, and their love being so perfect as to result in a person equal to dignity also, Rahner moves decisively away from what was fruitful to the Greek mind to a model which arises from our human situation and experience and specifically from interpersonal relationships. Mackey underlined that the danger of this is to reinforce our presumption that Christian theology is defining three persons in God in the sense that modern psychology thinks of persons. As long as we leave this danger clearly aside and understand that the concept is different, there is in Rahner's model a great deal of mileage for communications and counselling theology. Barth's self-differentiation in God as perceived in Scripture by faith, and Moltmann's social Trinity, can as easily be used as foundational material for a theology of communication and within that can be fitted the perspective of this counselling approach.

However we understand person, the theology of Trinity involves the proclamation of inner life within the Godhead and communication of that life to us in interpersonal relationships. What this means in practice for the Christian is that his or her relationships with Father, Son and Holy Spirit are at the human end quite distinctive relationships. We pray to the Father in the Son by the power of the Holy Spirit—as the liturgy provides in model. In these relationships, we receive life, grow in new life and come to fulfillment in perfect union: a union whereby God lives in us and we live in God. Perfect communication moves from and through symbol to reality. The theology of communication and therefore of counselling is essentially the modelling of human communication on God's: this demands of us listening, respecting, self-giving, caring and identifying, in a free movement towards a communion in which we retain our individuality.

Colin Morris distinguishes information from communication and this may well help us to distinguish between advice-giving and counselling. 'Information is the passing on of bits of intelligence; communication is about the self-disclosure of the communicator in the act of passing on bits of intelligence.' He alludes to George Gerbner's definition of communication as 'social interaction regulated by messages'.[55] We can approach this from two directions. One is to see that the ultimate aim of all communication is to reveal God in our midst. The other is to start at the human end and say that the divine process of self-communication is the model of what all true communication between human beings should be. A middle view would be that it is a bit of both. If we believe God became man in Christ and that we can find him in every other human being, particularly those in need, then opening ourselves for the other to unfold the mystery of his or her being to us will eventually enable us to find God there: On the other hand it may well be that it is only when we become

152

aware of how God gives us room to be wrong and is patient with us as he beckons us to come to him that we will have the required vision and sustained love to persevere through the more demanding counselling situations.

● ● ●

If this book helps one person to put aside the stone they were about to throw at one of God's 'bruised reeds' and listen instead to their pain and confusion, it will have been worthwhile. If this book helps Christian ministers and care-ers to listen before they speak, and walk with people's pain before they preach, a small but I believe crucial and significant contribution to Christian communication will have been effected. And at the end of the day, Paul's words about God choosing the weak things of the world and his encouragement to people to pray for those who preach to others that they don't become castaways themselves, must remain the consolation of any author venturing into the subject matter of this book.

Appendix

**Questions Raised for Non-Judgmental Counselling by
Attacks on Open Line**

DOES COUNSELLING contradict what Christians should be doing? It may seem strange to pose the question, but almost every radio programme or television programme in which non-condemnatory counselling has been used by priests has been attacked by good Christian people as betraying the true faith. There have also been rumbles about the counselling done by organisations like the Catholic Marriage Advisory Centre but since they have been discreet in their public pronouncements and are of course private in the actual counselling they do, attacks have been mostly confined to grumbles among the clergy at Deanery meetings and the like. In Chapter 2, we had Fr Jim McLaren speaking of how in his radio counselling work in Australia the right wing members of the Church constantly ask him 'Why didn't you tell them that it was a sin?' He replies very succinctly that the caller is not looking for a Church reaction or a theological answer but rather for Christian support and caring. This is not to preclude the theological or even the judgmental response but rather to say that there is a time and place for everything. Before there can be any theological dialogue there must first be established a relationship within which that dialogue can take place. Before we have the right to offer any judgment, we must first be asked for it: 'judge not lest ye be judged.'

My own experience of campaigns by Christian people claiming that non-judgmental counselling contradicts our responsibilities as Christians is extensive. It is a good illustration of the issues which every Christian and in particular every Christian teacher, minister or priest must wrestle with if they are to be true to both their professional obligations and their basic caring as Christians. As such it has much wider relevance and this has been recognised by thoughtful people. The Catholic priest representative on CRAC (Central Religious Advisory Committee) has put it in writing on several occasions that if the attacks on my work

succeed, every priest working in the media will be under immediate threat, for the media in Britain both under the BBC charter
and the IBA and its successor as a regulatory body have the
obligation of impartiality imposed as central to any professional's
use of the media. (This is in no sense a muzzle on the expression
of what one stands for or believes in but has to do with how one
expresses one's opinions: there must be no use of manipulative
techniques or taking advantage of privileged positions; and there
must be deep respect for the rights, views, dignity and sensitivi-
ties of the people listening or viewing. Similarly, a health service
professional from Lanarkshire wrote to a national Catholic
weekly to underline the fact that the principles of non-judgmental
counselling to which I subscribe are the only principles which
would allow any health service professional to so his or her job
within the National Health Service. Again too, the newly
developed task of guidance teachers in our secondary schools
imposes similar restrictions on the approach to the young person
in trouble. The resulting dilemmas mean that at the moment,
guidance teachers tend to get attacked by their teaching col-
leagues in Catholic schools as being too liberal, and attacked by
social workers as being paternalistic or unapproachable on the
one hand or too professionally untrustworthy on the other.

The attacks on my role on *Open Line* began with complaints
to Cardinal Archbishop Gordon Joseph Gray by the then
chairman of the Society for the Protection for the Unborn Child
in Edinburgh. His failure to convince the archbishop and the
archdiocesan authorities that I was evil (despite cathedral protests
which led to the police having to be called); and failure (despite
initial success with Cardinal Knox at the Pontifical Council for
the Family) with the Roman authorities complained to, led in
1985 to a sustained campaign in which money seemed to be no
object. The original complainant, who recorded every word I said
on *Open Line* and *View from Earth* and used selected highlights
out of context to make his case, was joined by an ex-communist
who for years had felt let down by the Church and had been
dedicating his money and journalistic skills in his own publications in an attempt to undermine the efforts of bishops and
clergy alike in Scotland to implement with traditionally Scottish
caution and care the developments called for by the Second
Vatican Council. These two joined by the principal of a right-

155

wing Protestant evangelical school who was already well known for extremist campaigns. The area was blitzed by thousands of pamphlets. They were handed out and put on car windscreens at national and archdiocesan gatherings, sent to homes, given out at church doors, distributed in the Free Church to which belongs the minister who worked with me on the programme (even upsetting her old father who is a distinguished minister in the same Church), and then sent to advertisers on Radio Forth asking them to withdraw their advertising. Readers of the pamphlet were encouraged to write to the Apostolic Nuncio, to Cardinal Gagnon at the Pontifical Council for the Family and to the Pope himself.

The pamphlet accused me of encouraging abortion, contraception, fornication, sodomy and paedophilia on the basis of my giving to active homosexuals, when asked for it, the number of the Scottish Homosexual Rights Group, and on the basis that even though I did not personally recommend the Brook Advisory Centre (which does not exclude abortion, and campaigns for values I do not subscribe to), people on the programme sometimes did. The pamphlet also attacked my work as an interviewer on the news-based magazine programme, *View from Earth*: when I put questions to interviewees for them to answer the accusations made against their position, it was suggested that the content of the questions was an expression of my own personal views.

It is an almost unbelievable story of the relentless persecution of my really rather insignificant little work in local radio. It is in my opinion, however, something more. It is a paradigm of the way destructive forces can be mobilised through conservative groups of very good and loyal Catholics when there is a determined campaign to undermine those who are in the outreach of the Church's work of making Christ's warmth and compassion tangible in the full spotlight of the global village of today. The pattern is being repeated in all sorts of areas in the world and for this reason I believe it is relevant to outline it here. I have read of priests in America being excluded for being involved in touch therapy groups and black Church groups; priests in Latin America for being involved in liberation struggles and priests in Africa for becoming too 'native'. Now, whatever the rights or wrongs involved, the pattern of building up exclusion pressure for those who explore new patterns of being Christ for others must be faced and debated by all who are concerned for the future.

This apart, the subsequent content of the condemnation of my work by the Pontifical Council for the Family raises a whole series of scriptural and theological issues which are relevant for all Christian care-ers. On 15 July 1988, one of the leading prota-gonists, a relative of one of the Canons in the archdiocese who has worked behind the scenes on the issue, phoned *Open Line* to take issue with what I had said the week before to someone who had been left with the AIDS virus after a broken relationship with a man whom she had hoped to marry. She had said that she felt unable to go to church because Christianity taught that AIDS was God's punishment for sin. I had reassured her that in the incident with the man born blind Christ had contradicted the accepted Jewish view that either his sin or the sin of his fathers must have been responsible for his blindness. God, as taught by Jesus, is not a God who inflicts physical illness or dis-ability as a punishment or as a mark of sin. I could have gone on of course to open out the full implications of all of Our Lord's dealings with lepers, for there too the theology is clear. The protagonist on the phone chose to disagree with this theology, claiming that it meant a presumption of God's forgiveness . . . and none of us dare presume.

This is typical of the approach. Incontrovertible general state-ments are made—which all of us would agree with—but no attempt is made to work out the logical connection between the general statement and the alleged implication. In this case, leav-ing aside the question of whether accepting that God wants us all to receive forgiveness and has said that like the loving Father of the prodigal son He will come more than half way down the road to enable us to achieve this, is to presume on God's forgive-ness or not, I was horrified to hear her next argument. This was thrust in, despite my making it clear that I was not going to argue religious matters with her in the context of a helping programme. Almost unbelievably for a Catholic in this day and age, she said that the story of Sodom and Gomorrah in the Old Testament was a teaching that God destroyed two cities 'because of sodomy'. When I said very simply that I could not accept her inter-pretation of that story, she shouted 'That's because you're a modernist' and slammed down the phone.

157

There are of course two separate issues in this:

(a) The meaning quite literally of the story of Sodom and Gomorrah in text and context, within the literary form in which it was written. Here the fact that the Church has moved far away from any position that the positing of literary forms is 'dangerous modernism' is seen to be not just a matter for academia but for pastoral practice. The existence of priests in the Church who still teach within the terminology and understanding they were trained in at college forty years ago is a problem we cannot afford to continue, if we are not as a Church to betray Christ's truth and Christ's care for the *anawim*, the suffering, the wayward, the weak or the sinful. I don't know of any respectable Scripture scholar in the Roman Catholic Church who would accept the view that the story means we must accept that God sent fire and brimstone on these cities because of the sin of sodomy. There is a wide range of interpretations and of meanings but nothing approaching this quite outrageous view of the God perceived in either Testament.

(b) The second issue leaves aside the question of what the story was written to teach and asks whether we have any right to intrude our views—no matter how right or how wrong they are—on someone so desperately afraid and bewildered as an AIDS victim, and to reinforce within that person in her loneliness in the quiet of the night the very idea she already had, namely that she in particular was cursed by God and that there was no place for her in the offer of forgiveness in Christ's transforming love as incarnated in that very Church she was frightened to approach. Surely there could be no conceivable objection to a counsellor or priest like myself concentrating on the simple fact that there was a welcome for her in the local church, and that she was in no way an outcast branded by God for sin who could not dare come to her local church for acceptance (and forgiveness) like the rest of us sinners? The time for any change of lifestyle and coming to terms with areas of real guilt would come, as it comes for all of us within the trust of the community of love, when that community has enabled us to come to a very real meeting with Christ.

Both these issues, but particularly the second, lie behind the condemnation of me by the Pontifical Council for the Family under the leadership of Cardinal Edouard Gagnon. Here another characteristic of such campaigns is seen to be crucial: some small pressure groups carefully study the character of the Cardinals with such immense responsibilities in the Vatican and present their case accordingly. In my case they spent a summer going round each Roman congregation in turn till they found a point of entry. In this the character of Cardinal Gagnon—and his great concern for what he sees as crumbling morality in the Church—is central to the situation. On 29 September 1983, in an interview with the right-wing campaigning newspaper *The Wanderer* (published in the US but distributed world-wide), surveying the world scene on taking up his Vatican post, he declared 'You have a much worse situation (than in the 1930s in Italy) and I think personally that the most important thing would be to change 90% of the teachers of moral theology and stop them from teaching. Because they are teaching basically principles which lead to the sexual abominations.' Has there been any clearer example of the syndrome whereby the old lady looks at the marching soldiers and says 'They're all out of step except my Jock!'? He went on to appeal to the laity to identify errors in their bishops and present a case to Rome. He even described the necessary tactics:

If in a diocese you cannot find five or six people who have the intelligence and courage to study a case, with the help of lawyers, and present it to the Holy See, then nothing will be done. But it has to be proved. . . . So you have to choose a few very clear-cut cases, and document them very well. It's not the number and in fact you can overburden. If the Holy Father has 2,000 things, he cannot, physically, go through them. So take the clearest things—and I think there are enough—and work on them.

One of the examples *The Wanderer* talked about was Archbishop Hunthausen who suffered such a campaign and had half of his episcopal powers taken away in favour of a Vatican implant. It was a long struggle before the archbishop was vindicated and the implant bishop removed. Cardinal Gagnon in the same interview gave a clear window on his attitudes. 'Even in Rome itself, things are often not done as the Holy Father would like, and whenever the bishops come to Rome, he tells them what he wants on morality and catechetics and so on. But he doesn't have prisons to put them in, so many go back and don't obey.' Rarely has an aside quoted with approval illustrated an attitude so clearly!

More importantly, however, the tactics perhaps quite unintentionally encouraged in right wing groups in the Church are remarkably similar to those of Militant with regard to the Labour party in Britain. They even have their own newspaper, the US based *The Wanderer*, which adopts all the tactics of he Militant newspaper. This seems out of place in the Church of Christ when we think of how he attacked the Pharisees and Saduccees for similar pressure group divisions and loss of perspective. They too were good people, indeed among the best and most dedicated in Jewish society. Here again the individual example highlights the way in which any grouping in the Church, by becoming a single issue party, can undermine the work of the Church at parish, diocesan, national or world-wide level. Individual people get hurt by the mass campaigns of condemnation, even when they are innocent. It is inevitable in politics, but did Christ not come to build a different kingdom? In this kingdom, the shepherd is prepared to leave the ninety nine and search for the one that is lost. The woman similarly leaves aside her coins. The 'bruised reed' must be cared for.

All this provides the background for the running condemnations of my role in the *Open Line* by the Pontifical Council for the Family under the leadership of Cardinal Gagnon. Shortly before his death, Cardinal Knox had apologised to Cardinal Grey for his original acceptance of the complaints forwarded by the pressure group. On 23 March 1987, Cardinal Gagnon issued the condemnation which has remained unaffected by the flood of contrary voices since. This condemnation—shaped by those who orchestrated the campaign—is based on general statements which are incontrovertible being used to justify particular applications which on wider analysis do not seem to follow. Thus:

> In any situation where a Catholic priest or counsellor is speaking on matters touching faith or morals, it is absolutely essential that total integrity of doctrine be not only maintained at all times but also seen to be maintained.

The next point continues:

> Compassion must be understood, offered and applied in the light of doctrine, and not vice versa.

This is axiomatic in Roman Catholic theology, since philosophically and theologically what we are, and what we are by God's grace must flow into all that we try to do. The twist begins with the application of this principle when it is conjoined to the presumption fed to the Council that conflict situations bring a conflict between manifesting both the truth and the compassion of Christ. This I do not accept, but in my response to the pamphlet I had made what I thought were unobjectionable statements about the way and the pace at which we introduce all the doctrinal aspects of a situation into a conversation. As will be clear from the earlier chapters of this book, I believe that it is immoral and unchristian to leap to judgment with troubled people and try to impose our views when they are still searching for a trust relationship in which to begin to cope with their problems. Quotations from my response are then, however, forced into the following conclusion by Cardinal Gagnon:

When a person seeking help is so unreceptive to the truth that even the slightest hint of it (by either word or omission) would be received by him or her as harsh, lacking in compassion, imposing one's values, etc., then it is a lesser evil to leave such a person with that negative (and perhaps distressed) state of mind than to leave an impression of condoning behaviour which is objectively contrary to the law of God. The common good must take precedence over the supposed or felt needs of individuals who may be unwilling or unable to tolerate the sting of truth.

In point of fact, on the programme I never condone behaviour which is contrary to the law of God. People continually phone and say 'I know that as a priest you don't agree but. . . . 'What is in question is the most effective way both to help the person and to share with them what you personally are convinced is 'the truth and the life'. Non-judgmental counselling is, for me and for most professionals involved in the caring services of this country, the most sensitive and the most effective way to do both. I reject absolutely the hypothetical case in moral theology where the individual would be sacrificed to the common good and left in a negative and distressed state of mind. I do not believe the Cardinal in question would do this himself in pastoral work when talking to real people and not imagining theoretical case studies.

Once again, we are taken back to the scriptural studies which this whole issue highlights as being critical for our living out of Christ's commission. Modern insights into the New Testament make it abundantly clear that Jesus often put himself willingly into situations where enemies could misunderstand him and use the situation to try to destroy both his moral character and the integrity of his doctrine. John's account of his encounter with the woman at the well in Samaria is of a situation where Jesus broke the moral code in talking to a woman in public and in particular asking a Samaritan woman for a cup of water. Even his disciples were shocked.

Time after time John's gospel uses a clear instruction pattern of misunderstanding: what we have in the text is the final resolution of what may well have taken a great deal of time. In having women and tax collectors in his travelling group of disciples, Jesus also caused moral scandal and gave grounds to his enemies to label him as teaching the opposite of what the law taught. He said he was coming to fulfill the law and not abolish it and yet he asked people on the Sabbath to break the law as it was then understood. Clearly it is not a question of Jesus breaking the actual law or moral code; but it is also clearly a case of Jesus allowing people—for a good purpose—to think he was breaking his Father's law.

Again too, his parables show a teaching method where Jesus allowed people to be scandalised by what he said so that they would go away, think over what he said and—if they were genuine searchers—come back for further teaching which would resolve the complications. It is highly significant that he uses this technique only with the powerful and never with the Old Testament *anawim*, that is the searcher, the sick, the disturbed and the poor. He rebuked the disciples for attacking those 'not of our number' for falsely teaching in his name, giving the principle that those who were not against him were for him. Now this principle stands in dramatic and clear contradiction to Cardinal Gagnon's all-out primacy of sound doctrine in conflict situations.

Furthermore, Christ made it plain that those who give even a cup of water in his name have captured the heart of the gospel—the rest of the sound doctrine can be filled in as time goes on. Some alleviation of distress by caring listening (and prayer that Christ might become apparent in that caring: which is the context of all that I do) is the cup of water in the *Open Line* which meets the immediate need but also opens the door for those helped to come back to ask for more teaching. That is my privileged experience on *Open Line* and the testimonies sent to the Pontifical Council have made it clear that the broad sweep of priests and lay-people in the local Church who have listened to and judged my work on *Open Line* have made it clear I never need to do my work at the expense of condoning behaviour contrary to the laws of God in any sense at all. They cannot all be wrong. What I am saying is that even if there are times when I cannot possibly cover all the doctrinal aspects of a situation and do not seem to have covered them all in one conversation—or even when I try and do so inadequately due to my human frailty—Our Lord's own teaching method and pastoral approach ease my conscience.

The hypothetical case (where the individual would be sacrificed to the common good) is one that need never arise and does not arise. In point of fact, there are far less dangers to truth in my work on *Open Line* than if I were attempting to outline in a teaching radio programme the full length and breadth of what Cardinal Gagnon calls 'the Church's certain and irreformable doctrine'. In this my own human inadequacy and the limitations of any mass communication would have to make me daily fearful. Christ himself wept over Jerusalem because people could not accept his message; he was exasperated time after time with his own apostles; what chance is there for the rest of us?

Our daily exposition of the Word of God at Mass must mirror both our confidence in the message we preach and our constant prayerful search both as individuals and as the Church to find words which will be vehicles of the ultimately inexpressible. As Paul says we are to be always aware of being merely earthenware vessels for the infinite treasure of God's Word. Only this sort of attitude will allow us to share in word and caring with the needy that we too are surrounded by human weakness and that we see only 'in a glass darkly'. Then our pointing forward to the day when we 'see God face to face' will come across as real. This sort of challenge I have to face also on my *View from Earth* religious programme, but not on the *Open Line*—which attempts no such thing and so should not be judged accordingly. In most cases, on the *Open Line*, there is only the opportunity of preparing the way

163

for such sharing of the faith, but this in itself is a deep privilege and a richly productive happening.

The next point made in the condemnation by the Pontifical Council for the Family is to argue from what I said in my response to the Edinburgh pamphlet about respecting 'those whose moral views are different from my own' and my making clear the fact that in a phone-in programme 'we are in the hands of what the caller will accept' (they'll just put the phone down!) and we must find a caring agency which offers or is perceived to offer 'the kind of help they would feel able to accept'. This is twisted into 'adopting the language of those who tend to see the issue in terms of one human opinion against another' and a claim that I therefore hold that 'providing subjectively-felt relief for the individual distressed caller takes precedence over the need to safeguard publicly the objective truth about the morality of abortion and homosexual acts'. Such arguments and old-fashioned anti-modernism paranoia were fought out at the Second Vatican Council and most of us hoped that they had been buried once and for all by the statements on human rights. Sadly, however, they are still the food and drink of the pressure groups whose activities this campaign highlights.

In tune with the Council, we must be clear that to speak of respect for the views of others is to affirm our respect for the persons who hold those views. This is both the heart of the Incarnation and of the Council's declaration on inalienable human rights in the document on the Church in the Modern World. It is not to accept that merely human opinions can be set against revealed truth: revealed truth is the very foundation of membership of the Church. By it, I try to live; strengthened by it in prayer I try to live by it on the *Open Line*. So also must we all in our pastoral ministry; and so in particular must every Christian counsellor or care-er. In Britain we are fortunate to live in a society where the views of the Roman Catholic Church on abortion and homosexuality are clear to everyone within or outside the Church. Because of that it does not need to be repeated day in and day out. It can be and is presumed. Listeners know my views and when they want any reassurance, they ask . . . and I tell them. If we lived in a society where there was any doubt about where we stand, we would have to spend more time on communicating our positions. Where we have to do the work is in clarifying the care-ing which lies behind the doctrine. When people encounter it as they do on *Open Line* they are drawn to re-examine the doctrine they had previously rejected or dismissed without real consideration.

In the document of the Pontifical Council there is even an attempt to twist the way I used the incident of the woman taken in adultery to illustrate how we should not encounter the 'bruised reeds' with words of condemnation. It attempts—as the material fed to the Council did—to niggle at the meaning: 'Indeed, Jesus did not condemn her [though he did judge her, because he concluded with the words 'Sin no more'].' This niggle is to miss the whole point. It is not a matter of an isolated teaching incident but of Our Lord's whole teaching.

One need only read again Matthew's gospel and the parallel passages in Luke and Mark. In Mt. 7, we have the clear passage about not judging others so that God will not judge us. In Mt. 8 and 9 it is the outsiders, the centurion's servant, the leper, the blind and dumb, the official and the woman with the haemorrhage who are singled out for healing. When the twelve are sent out, they have to say what they have to say. If it's accepted, fine; if not, they should just walk on. Come to me, he said, all you who are weary and over-burdened and I will give you rest. In the sabbath controversy he quotes scripture: 'And if you had understood the meaning of the words: *What I want is mercy, not sacrifice*, you would not have condemned the blameless. For the Son of Man is master of the sabbath.' (Mt. 11:7–8)

St Luke's gospel is even clearer with his unforgettable picture of the gentle love of Christ, his sensitivity and his identification with the weak and suffering, with the outsider in whatever guise that outsider appears in Jewish society. And then there are the beautiful parables of forgiveness with God coming more than half way down the road to meet the sinner. The incident described in John of the woman caught in adultery is paralleled in Luke by the incident showing the contempt of Simon the Pharisee for the woman whom Our Lord should have known was a sinner.

Christ identified with sinners in such a way that he was condemned for it by all the religious powers in the land. That is the context for his challenge to the assembly gathered to carry out the sentence by stoning to death the woman caught in adultery. The parallel with the *Open Line* is clear, for everyone knew the woman was guilty and should not sin any more. The question was the condemnation and the stoning—physical or verbal. The history of the incident's place in the gospel underlines its teaching function. It is, however, part of the gospel and clearly part also of ancient tradition. Eusebius (H.E., 111, xxxix,16) sets it down that Papias 'records another story also, about a woman, accused in the Lord's presence of many sins, which is contained in the gospel according to the Hebrews'. The 'many sins' of course are different. In the third century Apostolic Constitutions 11, 24, a similar story is used to caution bishops against too great severity in dealing with penitents: 'The elders set before him another woman who had sinned, handed the decision to him and went out. But the Lord, who knows men's hearts, inquired of her whether the elders had condemned her. When she said "no", he said to her, "Go then: neither do I condemn you".' This may have been from the gospel of Peter. Thus scholars suggest it may have been inserted into John's gospel to illustrate Jn. 7:24 (Do not keep judging according to appearances . . .) and Jn. 8:15 (You judge by human standards; I judge no one . . .) or the sinfulness of the Jews contrasted with Jesus' sinlessness (Jn. 8:21, 24, 46).

In that context, I see it as clear vindication of the appropriateness of non-judgmental counselling as used on the *Open Line*, but also by every professional prepared to work within the National Health Service or the Social Work scene in Britain. The importance of their work makes this documentation necessary.

The final argument in the Pontifical Council's condemnation is that 'silence signifies consent by the presenter of a programme accepting that a colleague makes recommendations to the Brook Advisory Centre (which after counselling will not refuse to pass on to the doctors those who are determined on having an abortion) or the Scottish Homosexual Rights Group, in his own presence and with no trace of negative evaluation of the advice.' Now if this were the case, no contributer to a newspaper could continue if the editorial or feature material were not upholding Christian doctrine. The argument is, however, clearly based on ignorance of public service broadcasting as it exists in Britain— and this is perhaps understandable at the Roman end though not with the British campaigners. The presenter of a programme on public service broadcasting such as we have in Britain is in a quite different position from Vatican Radio or a Catholic

166

Broadcasting Service and is forbidden by contract and by licence law to impose his or her own views on a contributor. Silence does not signify consent any more than does a presenter putting the other point of view in a question suggest to the listener anything about the views of the presenter. The audience expects a presenter to be fair in enabling others to present their position.

Paradoxically, experts in both broadcasting and counselling talk at great length about how silence can be the most powerful and persuasive instrument for expressing disagreement, disapproval and an invitation to the listener to reflect further and look for other answers—an invitation which I try to give in season and out of season for that further searching. The skill of using silence for this purpose in broadcasting and in counselling is a skill which is recognised as difficult to learn.

At this stage it will probably be useful to move from the original condemnation by the Pontifical Council for the Family to the latest reaffirmation of that condemnation by Cardinal Gagnon. To put it into context, he had written in between times—in response to more pressure on him from the pressure groups—to the complainants, appealing to them on 10 November 1988 to begin a campaign of prayer and penance 'both to change certain hearts and to make reparation for the many scandals being perpetrated' and requested them to circulate his letters in the archdiocese to 'combat the campaign of vilification and calumny and of even more serious offences against this Office and the Holy See'. How the Archbishop of St Andrews and Edinburgh reacted to this attack on him in his own archdiocese can only be imagined.

The situation was made even more sinister by a series of three articles in *The Wanderer* which—with the clear encouragement and cooperation of the group if not Cardinal Gagnon's office itself—attacked first myself; then Cardinal Gray and Archbishop O'Brien; and then the Papal Nuncio, Archbishop Barbarito, not only for his support for me and Archbishop O'Brien but also for the episcopal appointments which were made while he was representing the Pope in Australia. All this has made it clear that the issues at stake are those which divide people who adopt positions similar to those of Archbishop Lefebvre and those who listen to and try to live up to the Second Vatican Council. It would be easy to dismiss the matter as an unfortunate combination of circumstances and say it arose simply because Cardinal Gagnon was personally disappointed that Archbishop O'Brien went back on his original promise of 29 August 1985 when he confided to Cardinal Gagnon: 'I do hope to bring his involvment in the programme to an end.' Any personal reasons for the continuance of the pressure on the local Church have now become almost irrelevant, as has my personal position also. This is why it must be opened out to public debate—which the National Council of Priests in England grasped so clearly in 1988 that they offered support to me almost unanimously. That gesture is one I will always treasure and it has given me courage to continue to stand within the Church for the principles involved.

The most recent charges were forwarded on 20 April 1989 to the Pontifical Council for the Family and are based on a document entitled 'objectionable material recorded October-December 1988' said to have been composed by a 'consultor to the Pontifical Council'. During this period of seven weeks there were approximately 540 contacts by phone or letter: of these the critic has been able to assemble only seventeen which are in his or her view morally permissive. The accusations are that my counselling partner on the *Open Line* recommended the Brook Advisory Centre and the Gay Switchboard and that I thanked her at the end of her advice. This is interpreted as approval of immorality. Now in my opinion to say that the normal civility of saying 'Thank you' implies approval is at best clutching at straws for condemnation; it also ignores what is normal practice in broadcasting. It was interesting that my partner was rebuked at the same time by a listener because she was forgetting to extend to me the same courtesy of 'Thank you' which I always extended to her!

To discuss the subject properly would mean the discussion of complex questions about the ways in which we should relate to helping organisations whose ideals in many respects are not ours but which have common cause with us in vast areas of human need. In terms of this controversy, however, what is presently significant is that I have agreed over the years not to make any referrals to these organisations because they are two-faceted—and this even when the referrals would be for purposes where the conflict of principles and moral values would not be relevant. One aspect of each is campaigning for values and principles I would not accept. Their views on sexuality are not the views of the Catholic Church and so to prevent confusion I do not refer people to their services. This may well be wrong because—at least in Edinburgh with the existing staff—both of them are reputable organisations staffed by caring people.

The views of the organisations by design and in practice do not destroy the impartiality of their counselling. They often refer young people to their Churches to talk about the moral questions which trouble them, because that is by definition part of the counselling process. It is difficult for those who live within the parameters of seeing only an authoritarian teaching Church to appreciate that such groups believe it is immoral to impose their views on anyone, but this is in fact the integrity they live by. It is undoubtedly true that the Brook Advisory Centre has rescued many young girls from the brink of suicide (many from good Catholic homes who were frightened to talk to anybody else), and that the Gay Switchboard has similarly rescued young people from suicide when all others had failed and has enabled many others not to be trapped into a homosexual way of life either from loneliness or blackmail.

These organisations pose major challenges as to how caring our Church is and how open to young people to talk freely about the 'unacceptable', because unless they can talk freely about such issues there is no possibility of them seeing the attractiveness of the morally right. It is a fact that more 'good' girls become pregnant than 'bad'. It is a fact too that sex before marriage is the norm rather than the exception, as much among Catholics as among those who are not Catholics. There is no use pretending that this is not so. To face this and work within it to point to the higher value that lies in sex being the expression of 'I take you for better or worse etc.' and therefore something that should be kept for marriage, is not to betray Christ's ideal but to give it some chance to be heard in the clamour of contrary voices.

Thus on 19 November 1988, I reinforced Valerie's dislike of her boyfriend's advances by getting her to ask herself why she was instinctively rejecting them. Step by step she was led to see for herself that the demands for sex were not love since the first principle of love is to respect the other person's wishes and values. For this I was accused of using purely subjective moral principles whereas I was trying to encourage moral development by helping

169

people to begin from where they were at that time and from the moral insights they were capable of perceiving at that time, and then working from that point towards a vision of the very moral principles which if laid down dogmatically before the listening world would have themselves blocked the moral development which was in fact slowly achieved. Valerie ended the conversation by deciding to end with her boyfriend in the light of her new view of the wider values involved in a relationship. About the same time Leanne was slowly being encouraged by my partner to start talking to her parents, when she was phoning because she was worried about being pregnant from sex in her home while her Mum and Dad were away on holiday. She was frightened and so, rather typically, rejected every suggestion Sheila made: the end result was that Sheila was accused of encouraging the very sexual relationships and the break between Leanne and her mother which she was slowly trying to counteract.

Then again it is a fact that some people are locked into homosexual feelings they can do nothing about, at least for the moment. This is a morally neutral situation in the strictest interpretation of the Church's teaching. What these people do about it in their constricted situation is the question of conscience. When that question is asked I make clear the view of the Catholic Church. There were times in the past when I referred people to the Gay Switchboard when they asked for the number of such an organisation. I do not do that now—lest the appearance of condoning active homosexuality is given to those who wish to take it that way—but there are circumstances in which I probably should. I certainly cannot interfere with the judgment of another professional counsellor who makes such a referral: the motive is not to encourage the spread of homosexuality but to help those who are in a very difficult situation.

The most difficult situation for me is when a young girl phones asking advice in pregnancy outside of marriage. I do not normally deal with such calls for I believe support comes better from a woman in such circumstances; when I have to deal with them I refer to the Innocents as well as Lifeline or Family Care. Other counsellors may well refer to the Brook Advisory Centre. Mostly this will be for advice about sexual relationships or personality problems but on the rare occasion it will be in pregnancy. This is a problem because of the campaigning side of the organisation which argues for a woman's right to choose and then have free access to abortion. The saving grace of the organisation is their principle of non-directive counselling even in such situations. They will refer on to pro-life groups or to a priest when the client gives indications that this will be helpful.

Even in the worst case, namely the girl who asks for help to have an abortion, a referral to the Brook Advisory Centre could even be justified in strict Roman Catholic theology on the principle of double effect. If the girl goes to the family doctor she will be offered an abortion within the NHS in Edinburgh without any counselling to clarify her decision. In the Brook Advisory Centre, the girl will at least get counselling and the opportunity to become aware that the termination is not the simple solution she imagines it to be, and that the destruction of life is involved, with subsequent problems of guilt and bereavement to be faced. On the principle of double effect, the good effect is that in this way she will at least be presented with the arguments against abortion and helped to keep her child if that is what she decides. The bad effect is clearly that some of those counselled may at the end of the day be helped to go to the doctor to see if they will be allowed an abortion. To sum up then: there are arguments to be discussed even in the position of those counsellors who might suggest the Brook Advisory Centre to those girls who refuse to talk to their parents. Whether they are right or wrong, however, I cannot interfere in their judgement. For myself I continue not to make referrals which could convey a confused image.

My sadness in knowing that an abortion may take place is not, however, unique. Every person involved in this area within the National Health Service may refuse to make a referral themselves but must pass on the girl to someone who will. This is not co-operating in evil any more than I co-operate in evil, and to pretend that it does not happen is to be like the proverbial ostrich hiding its head vainly in the sand. No answer—rather than an answer in these directions—would precipitate a back-street abortion rather than give the girl a chance to think again and be shown the way to alternatives which at first seem impossible to her.

Attacks continue but the balance is provided by support from the vast majority of the popultion and the vast majority of priests and people in the Church. I have treasured letters of

171

support from Fr Oliver McTernan of CRAC and the National Council of Priests in England. Special to me also was a unanimous vote of confidence and a letter from the priests in my own Deanery to the Nuncio. It would be very difficult indeed to work on *Open Line* without the prayers and solidarity of those who like me are entrusted with making Christ's voice and caring tangible:

> As his fellow priests in the Deanery he belongs to, we wish to put it on record that we recognise the difficulties under which Fr Monaghan labours in the particular circumstances of this programme. We appreciate his caring attitude and his untiring efforts to witness to the teaching of the Church. We thank him for the invaluable service which he renders to the community.

A secular radio critic in the Scotsman in 28 January 1989 gave a moving and totally independent evaluation:

> An *Open Line* in the wrong hands could indeed be bad, but Radio Forth's *Open Line* team, Andrew Monaghan and Sheila, do as well as anyone could be expected to do in their roles as counsellors. That is not to damn with faint praise: on the contrary. Giving a sympathetic ear is, in fact, not an easy thing to do: you have to make the right response—and that is extraordinarily difficult. The only thing that's predictable about the *Open Line* is that you can never exhaust the infinite variety of troubles that people can have, difficulties they can get themselves into. And there's no recipe for dealing with a multiplicity of poeple.
>
> On last week's programme, Fr Monaghan talked about the privilege of the *Open Line*. That attitude is what makes it all possible, makes it all right: the genuine belief that it is a privilege to be the ready ear, the punch-bag for uncontrollable anger, the handkerchief to dry a tear. Monaghan is himself in a difficult situation: the counsel he has to give has brought him into direct conflict with Catholic authority. For, as a supportive letter he read out said, he has to 'live in the real world', has to respond to deal with the situation people are actually in, as opposed to the situation they ought to be in according to some moral lights. He shows enormous courage in sticking to the programme even though it might cost him

dear. But perhaps he would say that he is exercising his priest-hood—and clearly the courage involved in that is recognised and appreciated by his audience.

The other side of the story is that while the programme exposes us to the messiness of life, it also brings out the sheer goodness of folk, how much we truly need each other, that no man, nor woman, can ever be an island. The *Open Line* is a privilege to listen to.

Another critic in *The Guardian* on 25 August 1989 listened to the *Open Line* for the first time and compared it with the similar programmes on the bigger radio stations in England. Here is an encouraging extract of what Ken Garner had to say:

There are desperate voices on the fringe of the Festival City. All of them were clearly in distress. Fr Andy gave them time. I know it's hard he said, it's going to be a desperately empty time for you. His strongest advice is: What do you think? Will you give it a try? He has the priest's bedside manner, but he means it. In the programme's early days, over a decade ago, a tasteless student audience listened in to laugh at the less fortunate and articulate. But Monaghan's resolve to be quiet-spoken and sympathetic saw them off. It would take a seri-ously puerile mind to find this distressing programme amusing.

In striving so hard to make good radio, the London prob-lem phone-ins might be going wrong. Debate, chat and a number of clashing voices sound exciting, so this is what we get. But the advice is irrelevant. It's the calling that matters. Listeners have their curiosity entertained by a drama made out of the caller's crisis. The radio counsellor, both script editor and director of true-life stories, is making dreams at the expense of someone's reality.

Andy Monaghan, however, has got it the right way round. He is the only listener here. Each caller knows themself to be the subject. For a time, this is their space. It's not the first person in this dialogue that is compromised, but the third party, the radio listener. Are we eavesdropping? Why tune in? The reason is, that although we may not yet know how to listen, after Fr Monaghan's lesson, we will have heard a man who does.

173

In a letter to the national Catholic newspaper I referred to earlier (*Scottish Catholic Observer*, 28 January 1989) Mrs Anne McKay opened out the issues detailed in this appendix to the wider pastoral work of the Church. I don't think there need be this conflict of standard, nor I suspect does she, but her realism is bracing:

> The matter, thought 'embarrassing' to the Church, nevertheless raises important questions for those working in Catholic counselling agencies today. The 'Which side are you on?' question would not arise if people understood the principles which underly good counselling. A counsellor is with his client: is trying to be empathic, non-directive and non-judgmental. Above all, he respects the client as an individual who makes personal choices and accepts responsibility. A Catholic counsels from the depth of his own suffering and in the power of the Resurrection.
>
> The interesting question arises to what extent a priest can operate these principles where perhaps 'souls' is preferable to clients and where he is also a guide and a teacher. Whether Fr Monaghan was attempting radio counselling or was merely giving advice, the Church knows exactly in which camp it expects its priests to be. 'Totally orthodox' according to Catholic Press and Media Officer Fr Tom Connolly, adding: 'He wouldn't be working as a priest if he was anything else.' Our Church recruits and helps to train many excellent lay counsellors, a fact not widely known. Presumably it would give them the same support it has admirably given Fr Monaghan— expecting total orthodoxy? The tension between 'toeing the party line' and meeting the requirements of the British Association of Counsellors is a challenge for the future. Fr Monaghan has resigned as Communications director to save his archbishop 'the embarrassment of these attacks'. The dispute may be diplomatically glossed over, but the question arising from it should not be ignored. It is to be hoped the Church will stay on the air and not retreat to the confessional.

Lastly, a letter to the Tablet on 1 October 1988 from the Catholic wife of the Church of Scotland Professor of New Testament studies at the University of Edinburgh gives some indication of the religious effectiveness of non-judgmental counselling as a pastoral outreach. Her testimony is more compelling in that she had never met or had any contact with me as a priest:

The programme reaches people who on the whole have no contact with any Church. They will trust 'Andy' (as Fr Monaghan is called on *Open Line*) with their problems though they would not dream of turning to a priest or a minister in their trouble. In Fr Monaghan they find a counsellor in a million. He is a listener rather than a talker; he enters into the suffering and grief of every caller so they know he understands; he never judges or condemns those who have made mistakes but helps them to see more clearly the consequences of their actions. He does not try to patch up the problems but points the caller to some other agency—very often the Marriage Counselling Service or the Edinburgh Association for Mental Health—where the distressed person will have a chance to talk through the whole matter over weeks or months. He never moralises or preaches but all that he says is informed with the Christian gospel. He has an extraordinary gift of being able to see beyond the first problem that the caller mentions to the much more serious underlying problem. And he has a sense of humour. He helps people to laugh or at least to smile.

I have often been impressed at the subtle change in approach when the caller tells him that he or she is a Catholic, whether practising or lapsed. He speaks then quite directly about Our Lord and his compassion; he speaks as a priest to a penitent; he makes it easier for that person to come back to the sacramental life of the Church and to find God again in prayer.

Perhaps the most striking thing about the programme is the intimacy and closeness of each conversation. It is often hard to remember that thousands of other people are listening. For Fr Monaghan and for the one in distress, all those listeners are forgotten and the conversation is personal and quite genuinely 'heart to heart'. But all the time, we who are listening are also learning. Light is shed on our own worries by these conversations we overhear. Fr Monaghan's assurance of God's love and forgiveness speaks to all. I often find myself wishing, as I turn off the radio at 2 a.m., that every priest and minister in the country could listen to the *Open Line* every

175

Saturday night. They would learn much. I do not know Fr Monaghan personally. But I, like many others, owe a great deal to his programme. In a country not entirely free of anti-Catholic prejudice, he has done much to assure that God loves and forgives and that a Catholic priest will listen to grief. The *Open Line* and its honoured reputation among ordinary people make me proud to be a Catholic.

That letter and countless others make me feel immensely honoured and privileged to be involved in the *Open Line*. It also convinces me that what it has taught me about relating to people is something we all have to learn in the Church if it is to relate effectively to people in the 'global village' of our modern world where so many are as isolated in their problems and relationships as they are immersed in knowing all that's going on around them. It is to that point of contradiction we must bring the individual healing love of Christ which will reaffirm them in their importance for other human beings and assure them of their value in the eyes of God. Such is salvation.

References

Introduction (pp. 1–8)
1. Kübler-Ross, E. *AIDS, the Ultimate Challenge*, London: Macmillan, 1987.
2. Rahner, K. 'Jesus Christ', *Sacramentum Mundi*, Vol. 3, London: Burns and Oates; *Theological Investigations*, London: Darton, Longman and Todd, 1961-73.
3. Von Balthasar, H.U. *Herrlichkeit*, Vol. 1, Einsiedeln: 1961.
4. Evely, L. Quotations throughout the book are from his popular writings such as *We dare to say Our Father, We are all Brothers, The Word of God, Joy, Joy and Suffering, The Prayer of a Modern Man, The Faith of a Modern Man, A Religion for our Time*, London: Burns and Oates, 1967-1970.
5. Bredin, E. *Disturbing the Peace*, Dublin: Columba Press, 1985.
6. Quoist, M. Quotations throughout are from *Prayers of Life, The Christian Response, Meet Christ and Live, Christ is Alive*, Dublin: Gill and Macmillan, 1970-1973.
7. Jones, C.W. *Listen Pilgrim*, London: Darton, Longman and Todd, 1968.
8. Evely, L. Cf. note 4 above.
9. Kennedy, E. *On Becoming a Counsellor*, Dublin: Gill and Macmillan, 1977.
10. Adler, R.B. and Towne, N. *Looking Out, Looking In*, New York: CBS College Publishing, 1984.
11. Clinebell, H.J. *Basic Types of Pastoral Counselling*, Nashville: Abingdon Press, 1966.

Chapter 1 (pp. 9–49)
1. Malraux, A. *Man's Estate*, London: Penguin Books, 1961, quoted by Boros, L. in *The Moment of Truth*, London: Burns and Oates, 1965.
2. Cf. Introduction note 2.
3. Ahern, B. *New Horizons*, Leominster: Fowler Wright Books (Dome), 1965.
4. Parkes, C.M. *Bereavement: Studies of Grief in Adult Life*, London: Pelican, 1972. (Also Kübler-Ross, E.)
5. Dominian, J. *Depression*, London: Fontana Books, 1976, pp. 149-50.

6. Hugget, J. *Listening to Others*, London: Hodder and Stoughton, 1988.
7. Clinebell, H.J. op. cit.
8. Grossouw, W. *In Christ*, London: Geoffrey Chapman, 1960.
9. The Bishops of the Netherlands, *A New Catechism*—with supplement, London: Search Press, 1970; translation 1967 and 1969 Herder K.G. and Burns and Oates.
10. Kelley, K.E. (Ed.) *Guilt: Issues of Emotional Living in an Age of Stress for Clergy and Religious*, Whitinsville: House of Affirmation, 1980.
11. Powell, J. *Why am I afraid to love?* Chicago: Argus Publications, 1970.
12. Martin, C. *Don't be afraid to say you're lonely*, London: Collins, 1987.
13. Dickens, M. and Sutcliffe, R. *Is anyone there?* Harmondsworth: Puffin Books, 1978-86.
14. Norwood, R. *Women who love too much*, New York: Avon Books, 1985.
15. Dalrymple, J. *The Christian Affirmation, Costing not less than Everything, The Longest Journey*, London: Darton, Longman and Todd, 1971-1979.
16. *The Code of Canon Law* in English translation, London: Collins Liturgical Publications, 1983, Canon 1184.
17. Kennedy, E. op. cit.
18. Engel, G. quoting *Psychological Developments in Health and Disease*, Philadelphia: W.B. Saunders, 1972; *Bulletin of the Menninger Clinic*, 1968.
19. Steinzer, B. *The Healing Partnership*, New York: Harper and Row, 1967.
20. Pretzel, P. *Understanding and Counselling the Suicidal Person*, Nashville: Abingdon Press, 1972.
21. Watt, A. *Nature, Man and Woman*, London, Sphere Books, 1976, p. 145.
22. Campbell, A.V. *Rediscovering Pastoral Care*, London: Darton Longman and Todd.
23. Vatican 11, *Pastoral Constitution on the Church in the Modern World* (*Gaudium et Spes*), 48ff., also the *Dogmatic Constitution on the Church* (*Lumen Gentium*) 11, 35, 41.
24. Luther, M. *Sermon on the Estate of Marriage*. Col 1 works, Vol. 44 pp. 1-14.
25. Gheon, H. *The Secret of the Little Flower*, London: Sheed and Ward, 1934.
26. Spring, J. *Cry Hard and Swim*, London: Virago Press, 1987.

27. Simpson, M.A. *The Facts of Death*, New York: Prentice Hall, 1979.
28. Pagan, A. *God's Scotland*, Edinburgh: Mainstream, 1988.
29. Rowe, D. *The Construction of Life and Death*, 1989.
30. Kirkpatrick, B. *AIDS: Sharing the Pain*, London: Darton, Longman and Todd, 1988.
31. Clarke, P.A.B. *AIDS: Medicine, Politics and Society*, Lester Crook Academic 1988, as quoted in 30).
32. Bishops of London Dioceses, *Ad Clerum*, April 1987.
33. Cotter, J. *What Price Healing in a Time of Epidemic?* Exeter: Cairns Publications, 1987.
34. Kübler-Ross, E. op. cit.
35. Flood, Dom E. *The Divorced Catholic*, London: Fontana, 1987.
36. Catoir, J.T. *Catholics and Broken Marriage*, South Bend, Indiana: Ave Maria Press, 1979. Also Häring, B. *No Way Out?* Slough: St Paul Publications, 1989.
37. Vanier. J. (many of his writings but here especially) *Man and Woman He made them*, London: Darton, Longman and Todd, 1985. Also Nouwen, H. *In the Name of Jesus*, London: Darton, Longman and Todd, 1989.

Chapter 2 (pp. 50–79)
1. *Pastoral Instruction on the Means of Social Communication*, Pontifical Commission for the Means of Social Communication, 29 January 1979.
2. Phelan, J. *Mediaworld*, New York: Seabury Press, 1977, p. 64.
3. McArthur, C. *Television and History*, B.F.I., 1978.
4. Falconer, R. *Message, Media, Mission*, Edinburgh: St Andrew Press, 1977.
5. Greeley, A. *Lord of the Dance*, London: W.H. Allen, 1984.
6. *Media Development* Vol. XXX 3/1983.
7. Mcleish, R. *The Technique of Radio Production*, London: Focal Press, 1978.
8. McLeish, R. op. cit.
9. Bonhoeffer, *Life Together*, New York: Harper and Row, 1959.
10. Frank, J.D. *Critical Incidents in Psychotherapy*, Baltimore: Johns Hopkins Press, c/ 1962, p. 249.
11. Hurding, R.F. *Restoring the Image*, London: Paternoster Press, 1980.
12. Hambly, G. *Telephone Counselling*, Melbourne: The Joint Board of Christian Education of Australia and New Zealand, 1984.
13. Powell, J. *The Secret of Staying in Love*, Chicago: Argus, 1974.
14. a) Erikson, E. 'Growth and Crisis of the 'Healthy Personality" in *Personality in Nature, Society and Culture*, Kluckholm and Murray Eds, New York: Knoff, 1956

b) Rapoport, L. in *Crisis Intervention: Selected Readings*. Howard J. Parad Ed., New York; Family Service Association of America, 1965.

15. Caplan, G. *Principles of Basic Preventive Psychiatry*, New York: Basic Books, 1964.

16. Carkhuff, R. *Helping in Human Relations*, New York: Holt, Rinehart and Winston, 1958.

17. Hambly, G. op. cit.

18. McLeish, R. op. cit.

19. Rosenblum, L. 'Telephone Therapy', *Psychotherapy: Theory, Research and Practice*, Vol. 1, p. 241.

20. Switzer, D.K. *Breaking Point*, London: Geoffrey Chapman, 1974.

21. McLeish, R. op. cit.

22. Jones, W.A. 'The A-B-C Method of Crisis Management', *Mental Hygiene*.

23. Rowe, D. op. cit.

24. Clinebell, H.J. op. cit. p. 152ff

Chapter 3 (pp. 80–118)
1. Kennedy, E. op. cit.
2. Switzer, D.K. op. cit.
3. Buchanan, D. *The Counselling of Jesus*, Hodder and Stoughton, 1985.
4. Adams, J. *Competent to Counsel*, New York: Presbyterian Reformed Publishing Co., 1970.
5. Buchanan, D. op. cit.
6. Ferder, F. *Words made Flesh*, South Bend, Indiana: Ave Maria Press, 1986.
7. Alder, R.B. and Towne, N. op. cit.
8. Gibran, K. quoted by Adler and Towne, cf. 7. above.
9. Clinebell, H.J. op. cit.
10. Grigor, J.C. *Grow to Love*, Edinburgh: St Andrew Press, 1980.
11. Matthew, S. and Lawson, K. *Caring for God's People*, Edinburgh: St Andrew Press, 1989.
12. Wyngaards, J.W.M. *Communicating the Word of God*, Great Wakering: McCrimmon, 1978.
13. Dillinstone, F.W. quoted by Morris, C. in *God in a Box*, Chapter 11.
14. Roguet, A.M. article in *Doctrine and Life*, Dublin: Dominican Publications, July/August 1959.
15. Jeremias, J. *The Parables of Jesus*, London: SCM Press, 1972.
16. Hovdia, R.W. *Worship*, 1967.
17. Clarke, E. *Sounds Effective*, London: Geoffrey Chapman, 1969, p. 55.

18. Connolly, B. 'Preaching, Problems of Communication', article in *The Furrow*, Maynooth: February 1966.
19. Magee, B. and Jones, P. *Intercom*, Dublin: March 1984.
20. Katz, E. and Lazarsfeld, P. *Personal Influence*, Glencoe, Illinois: Free Press, 1954.
21. Rahner, K. Cf. n. 2. Introduction.
22. Killinger, J. *Fundamentals of Preaching*, London: SCM Press, 1985.
23. Barth, K. *The Word of God and the Word of Man*, New York: Harper Torchbooks, 1957 p. 189.
24. Forsyth, P.T. *Positive Preaching and the Modern Mind*, Laden: Independent Press, 1857.
25. Nouwen, H. *Creative Ministry*, New York: Image Books, 1978.
26. Jackson, E. *How to Preach to People's Needs*, Nashville: Abington Press, 1956, p. 14.
27. Craddock, F. *As One Without Authority*, Enid, Oklahoma: Phillips University Press, 1971.
28. Beuchner, F. *The Alphabet of Grace*, New York: Seabury Press, 1970, p. 2.
29. Schweitzer, D. *Pastor, Preacher, Person*, Nashville: Abusdi Press, 1979.
30. Jowett, J H. *The Preacher, is Life and Work*, New York: George H. Doran, 1912, p. 133.
31. Morris, C. *God in a Box*, London: Hodder and Stoughton, 1984.
32. Vatican Council 11 *Declaration on Christian Education*.
33. Ferder, F. op. cit.
34. Rahner, K. Cf. Introduction note 2.
35. Goldman, R. *Readiness for Religion*, London: Routledge and Kegan Paul, 1965.
36. Freire, P. *Pedagogy of the Oppressed*, quoted by Groome, T.H. in his excellent book *Christian Religious Education*, New York: Harper and Row, 1980.
37. Ferder, F. op. cit.

Chapter 4 (pp. 119-153)
1. Rahner, K. 'The man with the pierced heart' in *Servants of the Lord*, London: Burns and Oates, 1968.
2. Garonne, G. *This We Believe*, Shannon: Ecclesia Press, 1969.
3. Boros, L. *God is with us*, London: Burns and Oates.
4. Evely, L. Cf. Introduction n. 4.
5. Bonhoeffer, D. op. cit.
6. Quoist, M. Cf. Introduction n. 6.
7. Brown, R. *Priest and Bishop*, New York: London: Geoffrey Chapman 1971.

8. Paton, A. *Instrument of Thy Peace*, London: Fontana, 1970.
9. Jones, C.W. op. cit.
10. Ahern, B. op. cit.
11. Quoist, M. Cf. Introduction n. 6.
12. Brown, R. op. cit.
13. Rahner, K. Cf. Introduction n. 2.
14. Cf. Baird, J.A. quoted by Bredin, E. op. cit.
15. Dodd, C.H. *The Parables of the Kingdom*, London: Cambridge University Press, 1938.
16. Jeremias, J. op. cit.
17. Bredin, E. op. cit.
18. Dulles, A. *Apologetics and the Biblical Christ*, London: Burns and Oates, 1963.
19. Morden, L. 'Miracle' in *Saramentum Mundi*, London: Burns and Oates, 1970.
20. Cf. Chapter 1, n. 9.
21. Küng, H. *On Being a Christian*, London: Collins, 1977, p. 237.
22. Bredin, E, op. cit.
23. Boros, L. op. cit.
24. Congar, Y. *Jesus Christ*, London: Geoffrey Chapman, 1966.
25. Durwell, F.X. *The Ressurection: a Biblical Study*, London: Sheed and Ward, 1960.
26. Schillebeeckx, E. 'Der Gott Jesu und der Jesus Gottes', in *Concilium*, 10, 1974. *God Among Us*, London: SCM Press, 1982.
27. Kennedy, E. op. cit.
28. Bredin, E. op. cit.
29. Congar, Y. op. cit.
30. Adam, K. *The Christ of Faith*, London: Burns and Oates, 1957.
31. Schoonenberg, P. *The Christ*, London: Sheed and Ward, 1971.
32. Gutwenger, E. The Problem of Christ's Knowledge, *Concilium*, 1966, 1/2.
33. von Balthasar, H.U. op. cit.
34. Moran, G. *Theology of Revelation, God Still Speaks*, London: Burns and Oates, 1967.
35. Rahner, K. Cf. Introduction n. 2.
36. Evely, L. Cf. Introduction n. 4.
37. Ferder, F. op. cit.
38. Buchanan, D, op. cit.
39. Schillibeeckx, E. *The Church with a Human Face*, London: SCM Press, 1985.
40. Hughes, G.W. *God of Surprises*, London: Darton, Longman and Todd, 1985.
41. Boros, L. op. cit.

42. van Breeman, P.G. *As Bread that is Broken*, New York: Dimension Books, 1973.
43. Buchanan, D. op. cit.
44. Ferder, F. op. cit.
45. Nineham, D. *The Use and Abuse of the Bible*, London: Macmillan, 1976.
46. Webber, R. *God Still Speaks*, Nelson, 1981.
47. *General Catechetical Directory*, Rome, 1975.
48. Morris, C. op. cit.
49. Dulles, A. *The Church as Communicator*, Multimedia International, 1971.
50. Goethals, G. *The TV Ritual*, Boston: Beacon Press, 1981.
51. Gallagher, M.P. *Help my Unbelief*, Dublin: Veritas Publications, 1983.
52. Webber, R. op. cit.
53. Mackay, J. *The Christian Experience of God as Trinity*, London: SCM Press, 1981.
54. Rahner, K. *The Trinity*, London: Burns and Oates, 1970.
55. Gerbner, G. quoted by Morris, C. in *God in a Box*, ch. 11.